The
College Cookbook

Recipes *for* Students *by* Students

Nancy Levicki
and
Sheila Ingwersen

1st Printing October, 1985
2nd Printing November, 1985
3rd Printing January, 1986
4th Printing January, 1987
5th Printing October, 1988
6th Printing May, 1989
7th Printing July, 1989
8th Printing April, 1990
9th Printing March, 1991
10th Printing March, 1992

Published by NJL Interests, Inc.
Houston, Texas

Printed by
D. Armstrong Co., Inc.
Houston, Texas

Cover Design and Illustrations by Doug Gobel

In several recipes the students have used Trademark products as ingredients. Although substitutes can be made, the brand names are only used as a suggestion.

Introduction

These are those recipes that college students *like* to eat. From across the country students sent in over 200 recipes they like to eat and cook. These are simple, easy to prepare recipes that college students enjoy cooking and eating.

We've also included some party menus for those special college occasions—along with a Thanksgiving Dinner for those students staying on campus over the holidays.

The enthusiasm we experienced in putting together this book is best summed up in one of the many positive comments we received from students. Stephen Young from Dartmouth wrote, "the cookbook you're *concocting* sounds great and should be a *delicious* success. It ought to be an especially hot *entree* with Mothers whose sons and daughters are away at school. I know my own Mother worried constantly about my diet and if she ever knew the *rotten, malnutritious truth* of it, she'd have been bananas by now. She would have slept a whole lot better had she equipped me with a book like yours."

Thanks, Stephen, and all the other students for your support and enthusiasm. We hope all those Moms will agree they'll sleep better knowing their college son or daughter has *The College Cookbook* in *their* kitchen.

*Here are just a few of the many students who
are listed on the back cover of the book. This*

made this book happen! All the students' names
book is dedicated to you . . .

Table of Contents

HELPFUL HINTS

Marbles in a double boiler or tea kettle will warn you when the water has almost evaporated.

Store fresh mushrooms in paper bags, never plastic, to preserve whiteness.

Use a clean pair of pliers to hold food when grating. You can grate down to nothing.

Popcorn pops better when stored in a freezer container in the freezer.

To keep parsley, watercress, or mint fresh for several weeks, refrigerate after washing in a screw-top jar.

Store fresh tomatoes upside down in refrigerator to maintain freshness.

Ripen fruits and vegetables by placing them in a brown paper bag in a closed cupboard.

To keep nut meats indefinitely, wrap securely and place in freezer.

To crisp celery, green onions, or cucumbers, place in ice water for several hours with a slice of potato.

Instead of a bowl, use a hollowed-out red or green cabbage as the bowl for a dip. The next day grate the cabbage and toss with a good vinaigrette dressing.

Put a piece of charcoal in each section of an egg carton for an easy way of transporting charcoal to a picnic. Set fire to the carton. When the carton has burned away, you will have a good start to your fire.

Be sure salad greens are absolutely dry before adding the dressing or the dressing will not adhere.

Add a pinch of thyme to fresh carrots, a sprig of mint to green peas or ¼ t. of fresh marjoram to melted butter and pour over spinach.

Put avocado pit in avocado dip to keep it green.

Place a clove of garlic into store-bought salad dressing to improve flavor.

Variations on the Mundane Sandwich

Open-faced sandwiches allow the chef to be creative with left-overs or any variety of typical sandwich fillings:

1. Butter a slice of whole wheat bread. Top with scrambled eggs and a dollop of mayonnaise. Sprinkle with a dash of dill weed.

2. Butter a slice of whole wheat bread. Top with a slice or two of ham, a slice of canned pineapple, and a sliced hard-boiled egg.

3. Spread a slice of raisin bread with mayonnaise. Top with a piece of lettuce and turkey or ham slices.

4. Spread a piece of white bread with sliced tomato. Top with a slice of white cheese (Swiss) and a dollop of mayonnaise. Sprinkle with dill weed.

5. Spread a slice of whole wheat bread with mayonnaise. Cover with peanut butter. Add sliced cucumbers and sprinkle with dill weed.

6. Spread a piece of dark bread with cream cheese which has been softened with a splash of milk. Add sliced radishes and lettuce leaf.

7. Spread a slice of bread with mustard. Top with a slice or two of cheese and a slice of orange.

8. Mix together a dollop of mayonnaise with a dollop of catsup. Spread a slice of whole wheat bread with the mixture. Top with sliced turkey or chicken and a dollop of chutney.

9. Drain a ¼ c. of cottage cheese in a strainer. Spread on a slice of raisin bread. Sprinkle with additional raisins or nuts.

10. Mix together 1 stalk of celery, chopped, with 1 slice of cooked, crumbled bacon and a dollop of mayonnaise. Spread on a slice of dark bread.

SUBJECT:

APPETIZERS/ SOUPS & VEGETABLES

A Green & White Delight

1 16 oz. package of cream cheese
1 jar of your favorite Jalapeno jelly

1 box of Triscuits

Put cream cheese on a plate. Cover with Jalapeno jelly. Guests can help themselves to Triscuits with cream cheese and jelly on them. This is simple and also tastes great.

Tom Rollins   **Harvard Law School**

Quick Energy for Cramming on Sports!

½ c. peanut butter
½ c. honey

Non-fat dried milk as needed

Mix peanut butter and honey add enough dried milk to make mixture solid. Roll into bite size balls and pop them into your mouth. I eat these right before a soccer match! Makes about 1 dozen.

Jennifer Whitlock   **UCLA**

Chili Con Queso

1 small Velveeta cheese

1 small can Taco sauce

Melt cheese over low heat, add Taco sauce. Serve with chips or over vegetables. Serves 4-6.

Lisa Taylor   **St. Mary's College**

Midget Meat Loaves

½ lb. ground beef　　　　1 Egg, beaten
2 T. onion, minced　　　　Salt & Pepper, dash
½ c. bread crumbs

1. Mix all ingredients together in a bowl.
2. Lightly grease cups in a muffin tin and fill with meat mixture.
3. Bake 15 minutes at 450°.
   Serves 4.

(Your favorite meat loaf mix may be substituted.) When loaves are done, they lift out of cups easily.

Suzanne M. Zinn　　　　　　　**Colorado College**
University of Michigan

Popcorn

Basic recipe:

Cover bottom of pan with a thin layer of vegetable oil. Add a layer of popcorn. Cover pan with a lid. Pop corn while shaking pan continuously. Add Weight Watchers Butter for a nutritious snack!

Variations:

To the popped corn, add:

raisins, dates, dried apricots or any dried fruit
peanuts or mixed nuts.

To two quarts of popped corn, add ¼ c. of melted butter. In a small bowl mix together 2 T. sugar, ⅛ t. nutmeg, ⅛ t. cinnamon. Sprinkle sugar mixture over popcorn and toss carefully.

Lisa DiChiera　　　　　**Eastern Michigan University**

Spinach Dip

1 pkg. of Knorrs
  Vegetable Soup Mix
1 c. sour cream

1 c. mayonnaise
1 pkg. frozen, chopped
  spinach

Thaw, drain and squeeze excess moisture from spinach. Mix all ingredients and let sit overnight.

Serve with crackers, raw vegetables, or French bread that has been cubed, brushed with butter and garlic salt, and heated until warm.

Stephanie Moore   Oakland University

Chili Con Queso

16 oz. Velveeta cheese
5-7 "Nacho" sliced
  jalapeno peppers

3 tomatoes (chopped)
½-¾ c. picante sauce

Melt Velveeta till creamy. Add chopped tomatoes and chopped peppers. Mix in picante sauce until mixture is creamy. The amount of sauce used depends upon the juiciness of the tomatoes. Serve with Tostado chips.

Hope Bradberry   University of Tulsa

Mexican Pizza

Spread - 2 large cans Jalapeno Bean Dip
Mash 3 avocados with 2 T. lemon juice or
1 can frozen avocado dip
Mix - 1 8 oz. carton sour cream
     1 pkg. taco seasoning mix
     ½ c. mayonnaise
Top with - 8 oz. can sliced black olives
       2 chopped tomatoes

Spread bean dip on large plate. Layer sour cream mixture. Top with cheese, olives and tomatoes. Serve with tortilla chips.

Christina Codner   University of Houston

Mexican Taco Dip

½ pkg. taco seasoning mix
8 oz. sour cream
1 large can bean dip

1½ c. guacamole
1 T. mayonnaise
1 c. shredded cheese

Mix taco seasoning mix and sour cream together in a bowl. On a platter, spread the following ingredients; bean dip, guacamole, sour cream/taco mix. Top with shredded cheese. Serve with chips.

Anne Malinak   **Georgetown University**

Poncho Villa Dip

Layer in a rectangular Pyrex dish:

2 cans refried beans (Gebhardt's)
Guacamole - fresh made
Chopped green onions, black olives, chopped tomatoes
Green Chile sour cream dip or sour cream (if you use sour cream, instead of green chili dip, also add canned green chiles).
Grated cheddar cheese
Picante sauce - swirled over all (Put picante sauce on right before serving.)
Dip with Tostados.

Serves 8.

Ronnie Jacobe   **Princeton**

Poncho Villa Layer Cake

Layer in order in a glass bowl:

1 can refried beans
1 tomato, chopped
1 small can chopped black olives
1 small can chopped green chiles

1 can frozen guacamole, thawed
1 cup shredded cheddar cheese
6 T. picante sauce
1½ c. sour cream

Serve with Fritos King Size dip chips. Serves 8.

Lisa Platt   **University of Arizona**

Four Layer Dip

2 large cans bean dip
2 or 3 ripe avocados
2 pkgs. cheese
   (white or yellow)

1 16 oz. sour cream
1 jar black or green olives,
   sliced

First spread the bean dip out in pan. Then place the mashed avocados on top followed by sour cream, olives and cheese. Then serve with Nacho chips. Serves 8.

Missy Cason   **University of Florida**

Gretch's Guacamole

This is a favorite, or staple that keeps me going until I can get back to Houston!

2 large ripe avocados
1 ripe tomato
4 green onions
½ lemon, squeezed

Salsa, either medium, or
   hot. (if you're a true Texan!)
Pepper to taste

Dice onions, cube tomatoes, cube avocados, mix with a fork. (Don't blend; only imitation Mexican restaurants puree their quac!) Add salsa and lemon to taste. Pepper to taste. Serve in bowl or on lettuce, with *hot* chips — straight from the oven. (If you're in town [Houston], Tila's has the best chips around and you can take them out.) Serve with cold iced tea, or better yet — Margaritas and Sangria. Serves 8.

Gretchen Harnischfegar   **Princeton University**

Shrimp Dip

8 oz. Philadelphia cream
   cheese
2 t. lemon juice
2 T. catsup

1 t. onion juice
½ t. Worcestershire sauce

Blend all ingredients and add:

⅓ c. salad dressing
   (mayonnaise or Miracle
   Whip)

1 can shrimp, drained and
   crumbled

Serves 8.

Ann Sherwood   **Standford University**

Tortilla Rolls

10 large flour tortillas
3 8 oz. pkgs. cream cheese
(softened and combined
with:)

6 T. mayonnaise
4 T. grated onion
Picante sauce

Spread cheese mixture on tortillas, roll and refrigerate at least 1 hour. To serve: slice ½" thick; dip in picante sauce. Serves 8.

Lisa Platt   **University of Arizona**

Hot Cheese and Bacon Hors d'oeuvres

2 c. grated cheese
1 c. mayonnaise
2 T. minced onion

1 can minced black olives
Party rye bread

Mix together above ingredients. Blend till smooth; spread on party rye bread. Sprinkle cooked, minced bacon on top. Bake at 300° for 10 minutes; serve immediately. Makes 30.

Whitney Hawsey   **Baylor University**

Sausage Balls

(Ingredients should be at room temperature.)

Mix: 3 c. Bisquick
      1 lb. roll Owens
      Hot Sausage

10 oz. Cracker Barrel *extra
  sharp* grated cheese.

After combining ingredients, form bite size balls. Bake at 375° for 12 minutes or until brown on ungreased cookie sheet. Cool, then place in Ziploc Bags and freeze. Before serving, reheat at 300° for 10 or 15 minutes. Yield: 5-6 dozen.

Trey Wood   **Southern Methodist University**

Mini-BLT

1 pt. Hellman's mayonnaise	1 3.25 oz. bottle Baco's
1 pt. box cherry tomatoes	bacon bits
	1 lg. loaf white sandwich bread

Very lightly toast bread. Cut into 1" circles with cookie cutter. Spread on bacos, mayonnaise mix. Top with slice of tomato. Makes 6 dozen.

Linda Metz   **Texas Christian University**

Sliced Hotdog Appetizer

1 lb. hotdogs	1 jar currant jelly
1 jar French's mustard	

Cut hotdogs on angles and simmer for 2 hours in mustard and jelly. Serves 8.

Ann Sherwood   **Stanford University**

King Crab Dip

6 oz. cream cheese	3 garlic cloves chopped fine
1 T. milk	Splash of Tobasco sauce
4 T. chopped green onion	1 pt. fresh crab meat
1 t. horseradish	Grated Swiss cheese
¼ t. salt	Slivered almonds (optional)
¼ t. pepper	

Mix all ingredients except cheese and almonds. Put ½ mixture in a dish. Layer with cheese and almonds. Put in other half of mixture. Top with cheese and almonds. Bake at 375° for 15 minutes or until cheese melts! Serves 8-10.

Renee Madden   **Southern Methodist University**

Fried Cheese

1 10 oz. pkg. Cracker Barrel
    Sharp or Extra Sharp
    Natural Cheddar Cheese
    cut in ¾" cubes

2 eggs, beaten
¾ c. dry bread crumbs
1 T. sesame seeds

Dip cheese in egg, coat with combined crumbs and sesame seeds. Repeat until all cheese cubes are coated. Fry in deep hot oil at 350° for 1 or 2 minutes or until lightly browned. Serves 8.

Laurie Nuss   **Southwest Texas State University**

Parmesan Sticks (Extra Simple)

Slice pieces of white bread into four fingers. Dip in melted butter and roll in grated Parmesan cheese. Place on greased cookie sheet and bake at 350° until golden brown. Can be used as hors d'oeuvres or broken up for croutons.

Patty Bauer   **Georgetown University**

Sausage Surprises

2 lb. bulk sausage
½ c. bread crumbs

1 apple, peeled and finely
    chopped

Combine all ingredients and shape into patties. Brown in skillet over medium heat; drain well. Makes 12-14 patties.

Holly McKay   **Baylor University**

Hot Cheese Balls

1 lb. hot bulk sausage
3 c. Bisquick

10 oz. extra sharp cheese
Salt to taste

In a large bowl, mix all of the ingredients together using your hands. (If you can't remember the last time you washed your hands, please wear gloves.) Roll the mixture into small balls and place on a cookie sheet. Bake at 375° for 25 minutes.

This recipe makes 2 tons, so you better have room in the freezer for leftovers.

Paige Kreager   **Southern Methodist University**

Tom Holliman's Chili Con Queso

1 lb. Velveeta cheese
1 can Rotel tomatoes
1 can green chiles

1 white or yellow onion,
   finely chopped
1 clove garlic, finely chopped

Saute onions, garlic and tomatoes. Melt cheese; add green chiles. Serve with chips. Serves 8.

W. Scott Locher   **Stanford University**

Holiday Crab Dip

Blend together:

1 9 oz. pkg. softened cream
   cheese
1/3 c. mayonnaise

1 t. horseradish
1½ t. dried minced onion
½ t. seasoned salt

Fold in:

1 T. chopped parsley
Dash garlic powder

1 6 oz. pkg. king crab

Refrigerate for 24 hours *before* serving and keep refrigerated. Serve with holiday crackers. Serves 8.

Sheryl Durkee   **University of Mississippi**

Artichoke Dip

½ c. Parmesan cheese
½ c. mayonnaise

1 can artichokes (drained and chopped)

Mix above ingredients together. Mix in few drops of Tobasco sauce. Bake at 350° for 30 minutes. Serve with crackers. Serves 6.

Lisa Jewell   College of William and Mary

Skinny Dip

1 pkg. Hidden Valley Ranch dressing
1 c. low fat milk

1 c. Weight Watchers mayonnaise
Assorted vegetables (raw)

Mix above items then chill for 30 minutes. To be used as dip but sparingly. Makes 2 cups of dip.

Lori Valenti   University of Florida

Easy Baked Brie

Put desired amount of Brie in bowl in oven. Bake till bubbling. Serve on platter with apple, pear, bread slices. The key is in the design! It is a "quick" hit!

Gretchen Harnischfegar   Princeton University

California Quesadillas

1 avocado, sliced
4 T. grated Monterey Jack cheese

4 T. mild taco sauce
4 flour tortillas
Garlic salt (to taste)

On top of tortilla sprinkle cheese. Next spread taco sauce over cheese. Then place avocados on top. Sprinkle salt on tortilla and place in frying pan or microwave. Heat until cheese is melted. Remove quesadilla and enjoy! Serves 2.

Marie Barnett   University of Southern California

Puffy Cheese Wedges

2 eggs, beaten
1 c. flour
¾ t. salt
⅛ t. pepper

¾ t. oregano
1½ c. milk
8 oz. Munster cheese, grated
¾ c. chopped pepperoni

Mix egg, flour, salt, pepper, oregano and milk. Set aside ¼ cup cheese for topping. Add the rest of cheese and pepperoni to egg and milk mixture. Pour into a well-greased pie plate and bake for 30 minutes at 425°. Do not overbake. Sprinkle with remaining cheese and bake 2 more minutes. Cut into wedges and serve. Serves. 8.

Susan Smith   **Dartmouth College**

Fried PB & J

2 slices of bread
Peanut butter

Your favorite jelly
Butter

Spread the peanut butter and jelly on one slice of bread. Place the other slice (one side spread with peanut butter) on top. Got that? OK. Put butter on the outsides of the sandwich and place the sandwich in a heated skillet until each side is browned. Dig in!

Laura Neely   **Baylor University**

Cream Cheese Balls

Dried canned beef
Onion

Cream cheese
Tabasco (dash)

Shred beef - (Wisinact is easiest) - mix cream cheese, minced onion to taste, and dash of Tabasco. Make cream cheese into small balls and roll in shredded beef until completely coated.

Martha Harrington   **Stanford University**

Canadian Cheese Soup

¼ c. butter
½ c. finely diced onions
½ c. finely diced carrots
½ c. finely diced celery
¼ c. flour
1½ T. cornstarch

1 qt. chicken stock
1 qt. milk
⅛ t. baking soda
1 c. processed cheddar-type
  cheese, grated
Salt and pepper

Melt butter in large pot. Add onion, carrots, celery and saute over low heat until soft. Add flour and cornstarch and cook until bubbly. Add stock and milk and make a smooth sauce. Add soda and grated cheese, season with salt and pepper. Serves 8

Kelley Jones   **Georgetown University**

Broccoli and Cheese Soup

¼ c. butter or margarine
¼ c. minced onion
¼ c. flour

4 c. milk
1 c. Velveeta cheese
1½ c. frozen broccoli

Prepare broccoli beforehand until amost done - drain and chop. Melt butter in large pan. Saute onions in butter until tender. Blend in flour, cook one minute and gradually stir in milk, stirring constantly until thick and bubbly. Reduce heat. Add cheese a bit at a time, stirring until melted. Add chopped broccoli and heat. Serves 6.

Heather Hawkins   **Southwest Texas State University**

Eggplant Parmesan

2 medium eggplants
1 egg, beaten
¼ lb. butter

Italian bread crumbs
Tomato sauce
1 c. Parmesan cheese, grated

Slice eggplants into ¼ inch thick slices. Dip slices into beaten egg until covered. Then put slices into bread crumbs; cover on both sides. Place eggplant slices into a skillet with melted butter. Fry on both sides until golden brown. After frying all of the eggplant, place it in a Pyrex dish. Cover it with tomato sauce and then cheese. Put dish in oven and broil until the cheese bubbles or browns lightly. Serves 6.

Shayna Goldstein   **Southern Methodist University**

Creamed Onions

2½ lbs. small white onions	½ c. heavy cream
4 T. butter	¼ t. ground nutmeg
4 T. flour	1 t. salt
1½ c. milk	White pepper

1. To peel onions, drop in boiling water and boil for 30 seconds. Drain and cut off root ends and papery outer layers.
2. Drop onions in lightly salted boiling water so they are just covered.
3. Reduce heat to low and simmer, partially covered, for 20 minutes.
4. Drain the onions over a bowl and set aside. Measure and reserve 1 cup of the cooling liquid.
5. In a heavy 3-4 quart saucepan melt butter over medium heat.
6. Add flour and mix well.
7. Stir constantly and add reserved cooking liquid, the milk and cream. Cook over high heat until it comes to a boil, thickens slightly and is smooth.
8. Reduce heat to low and simmer 3-4 minutes. Stir in nutmeg, salt and pepper to taste.
9. Add the onions, turning gently with a spoon, and simmer until heated through. Serve at once from a heated bowl. Serves 8.

Heidi Sparks   **Syracuse University**

Squash Casserole

12 medium squash boiled in salt water until tender - drain

Mix the following and add to squash:

2 eggs	¾ c. grated cheese
1 onion, chopped and sauteed in small amount of margarine	½ can chopped green chilies

Bake at 350° for 1 hour in a Pyrex dish. Serves 8.

Teri Dale   **College of William and Mary**

Spinach/Broccoli Casserole

2 pkg. chopped broccoli or spinach (cooked and drained)
1½ c. chopped celery, cook til soft
½ stick margarine
½ jar Cheese Whiz (4 oz.)
1 can cream of mushroom soup
1 can water chestnuts, sliced

Combine all ingredients (an 8" sq. casserole dish is perfect) and bake in moderate oven 350° for 10-15 minutes. Serves 8.

Anne Worsham　　　　　　**University of Texas at Austin**

Zucchini Fritters

5 T. Bisquick
½ c. Parmesan cheese
2 c. grated zucchini
2 eggs
¼ t. onion or garlic flakes (or chive or celery flakes)
⅛ t. pepper
½ t. Italian seasoning

Blend Bisquick, cheese, pepper, onion flakes, and Italian seasoning. Add eggs and zucchini and blend in. Melt 2 T. butter or oil in pan. Drop batter from tablespoon. Fry for 3 minutes on each side. Serves 6.

Eleanor Hoppe　　　　**University of Southern California**

Single Vegetable Bake

Preheat oven to 350°. In an oven proof baking pan, grease the bottom with margarine.

Choose one: tomato halves, zucchini sliced lengthwise, green beans, or carrot sticks.

Put them in the dish. Sprinkle with crumbled cheese or cheese slices. Bake 20 minutes or until not so crunchy. Sprinkle with bread crumbs or sunflower seeds and stick under broiler briefly.

Libby Hyde　　　　　　　　　　　**Amherst College**

Chopped Broccoli Casserole

2 pkgs. frozen chopped
  broccoli, cooked and
  drained
3 eggs
1 c. bread crumbs

1 c. grated cheddar cheese
1 T. grated onion
1 t. sugar
1 can cream mushroom soup
  or cream of celery soup

Combine all the above and place in buttered casserole.
Sprinkle with bread crumbs. Bake at 325° for 20-30 minutes.
Serves 8-10.

Laurie Nuss   **Southwest Texas State University**

Broccoli Souffle

1 pkg. frozen chopped
  broccoli
½ c. mayonnaise
1 small onion, diced

½ can cream mushroom soup
½ c. grated cheddar cheese
2 large eggs, well beaten

Cook broccoli about 2 minutes *less* than package directions;
drain well (or thaw package at room temperature early in day
and omit cooking, but try to drain off excess water).

Mix soup, mayo, onions, cheese, eggs in lightly greased
casserole. Bake at 325-350° for 55-60 minutes. Serves two
generously. Goes with warmed rolls and a salad.

Janice Lodato   **Trinity University**

Broccoli Supreme

½ stick butter
1 onion chopped
2 pkgs. chopped broccoli,
  thawed

1 can cream mushroom soup
1 small jar Cheese Whiz
1 c. cooked rice
¼ c. slivered almonds

Saute onion in margarine, add broccoli and soup. Stir and
simmer, add cheese, then rice. Garnish with almonds. Bake
25-30 minutes in 350° oven. Serves 6.

Libby Layton   **Texas Christian University**

Broccoli Rice Casserole

1 pkg. frozen chopped broccoli	½ c. chopped celery and onion

Place in ½ c. water for about 10 minutes. Drain. Add:

1 c. cooked rice	1 can cream of mushroom
½ small jar Jalapeno Cheese Whiz	soup
	½ stick margarine or butter

Place in buttered casserole dish. Bake at 350° for ½ hour. Serves 5 to 6.

Robert O'Brian   Southern Methodist University

Broccoli & Rice Casserole

¾ stick margarine	1 can cream of mushroom
½ c. chopped onion	soup
2 10 oz. pkgs. frozen chopped broccoli	2 c. cooked rice
	1 c. grated cheese

Saute onions in margarine. Pour onions into bowl. Mix in thawed broccoli and rest of ingredients. Pour into a greased casserole dish and bake for on hour at 350°. Serves 8.

Nolen Dale   Trinity University

Curried Rice

1 t. curry powder	4 c. hot unsalted cooked rice
4 T. butter or margarine	Chopped parsley
2 T. chopped green onion	

In a saucepan cook onions with curry and butter until tender. Toss with rice and garnish with parsley. Serves 8.

Mancha White   Randolph-Macon Woman's College

Gator-Taters

2 potatoes
¼ c. butter or margarine
2 T. milk

Bacon bits to a desired taste
Cheddar cheese to a desired
taste - grated

Bake the potatoes for one hour or until skin is hard at 400°. Cut potatoes down the middle and scoop out the potato into a bowl and mix with butter or margarine and milk. After mixing, add bacon bits and stir. Put the mashed potatoes back into the potato skins and cover top of potato with cheddar cheese. Put the potatoes back into the oven for a half hour at 400°. Serves 4.

Julie Palmer   **University of Florida**

Potato Casserole

1 lb. frozen hash browns
½ pt. sour cream
1 small diced onion
1 can cream of mushroom
  soup

½-1 c. grated cheddar cheese
Dash of salt and pepper
1 box cornflakes (optional)

Mix ingredients. Put into greased casserole dish (8 in. sq.). If desired, crumble cornflakes over the top. Bake at 325° for 1 hour and 15 minutes.

Dinah Miller   **University of Texas**

SUBJECT:

MAIN COURSES

Pork Chops 'n Rice

4 large pork chops	1 can beef bouillion or
1 c. regular uncooked rice	consomme
	1 large onion, thinly sliced

Brown pork chops in small amount of oil. Pour rice in the bottom of casserole dish. Place browned pork chops on top of the rice. Cover with the sliced onions. Combine bouillion plus enough water to make a total of 2 cups liquid. Pour over chops. Cover. Bake at 350° for 1 hour.

Judy Raymond   **Southern Methodist University**

Ham Jambalaya

1 lb. cooked ham, cubed	1 garlic clove, crushed
about 2½ cups	1 16 oz. can tomatoes
½ lb shelled raw shrimp	1 13¾ oz. can chicken broth
5 bacon slices	1 bay leaf
1½ c. regular long grain rice	½ t. salt
1 medium onion, minced	½ t. thyme
1 medium green pepper, diced	3 to 4 drops Tabasco

About 1 hour before serving:

In large skillet over medium heat, fry bacon until crisp; drain on paper towels, crumble and set aside. In same skillet over medium heat in remaining bacon drippings, cook rice, onions, green pepper and garlic until rice is slightly browned. Stir in tomatoes and their liquid, chicken broth, bay leaf, salt and thyme. Cover and simmer 15 minutes. Stir in ham, shrimp and hot pepper sauce; cook, covered, 15 to 20 minutes until rice is tender, stirring occasionally. Spoon onto platter, sprinkle with bacon. If it seems too dry as it is cooking, add a small can of tomato juice.

Lamar Curtis   **Tulane University**

37

Sun Devil Surprise

1 lb. ground beef	Dash onion powder
2 T. soy sauce	Pepper
2 T. teriyaki sauce	Grated cheese
1 T. picante sauce	4 flour tortillas

Brown beef on high heat, drain, lower heat to medium. Mix in soy sauce, teriyaki sauce, onion and pepper. Put mixture on a warm flour tortilla, top with cheese and picante sauce and eat it. Makes 4 servings, takes 15 minutes.

Nancy Taylor   Arizona State University

Vegetarian Tacos

Stick preformed shells in toaster oven at low heat. Warm a can of Campbell's Brown or Black Beans (can't remember what they're called) on the stove and add chopped tomatoes and a dash of spicy sauce (Tabasco). Meanwhile, chop lettuce, onion, cheese. When beans begin sticking to the pan, take them off, stuff the shells with all ingredients and garnish with yogurt; better than sour cream.

Libby Hyde   Amherst College

Chili Gaetz

1 lb. hamburger	1 chopped onion

Saute and drain.

1 can tomato soup	1 can kidney beans plus juice

Add to the above.

3 T. chili powder (2 T for milder)	1 t. salt
1 T. flour	3 T. water plus a little more

Mix together into a paste and add to other mixture. Simmer 45 minutes. Top each serving with grated cheddar and chopped onion, if desired. Serves 4.

Susan Gaetz   Vanderbilt University

Hamburger Soup

1 lb. lean ground beef	1 bay leaf
1 c. cubed potatoes	6 c. water
1 can tomatoes	¼ t. basil
1 c. onions	4 t. salt
1 c. sliced carrots	⅛ t. pepper

Brown beef and drain; add onion and saute; add remaining ingredients; cook for 1 hour plus. Place in bowls and sprinkle with cheddar cheese.

Mary Bresnicky

Yale University
Notre Dame Law School

Potato-Beef Quick Meal

2 lbs. ground beef	½ t. Worcestershire sauce
1 c. chopped onion	1 pkg. of au gratin or
¼ c. chopped green pepper	scalloped potatoes
1 t. brown sugar	2 c. (16 oz.) tomatoes, chopped
1 t. salt	with juice
1½ c. water	½ c. shredded mozzarella
	cheese

Preheat oven to 350°. In deep oven-proof pan, brown ground beef, drain. Add rest of ingredients, mix and bring to boil. Bake 45 minutes at 350° or until potatoes are tender. Sprinkle with cheese. Bake until cheese melts. Serves 6.

Kelly Brown

Stanford University

Sloppy Joe's

Brown one lb. hamburger and drain.

Mix together:

½ c. chopped onion	1 T. vinegar
1 T. sugar	1 c. catsup
1 T. prepared yellow mustard	

Pour mix over browned beef. Simmer until onion is tender, 30 to 45 minutes. (Make mix in blender or chop onion in blender.) Serves 4.

Robin Sims

Southwest Texas State University

Leo's Chili-Mac

2 boxes Kraft Macaroni & Cheese
1 lb. ground beef
1 envelope Lawry's Chili Seasoning

1 stick butter
½ c. milk

Directions:

1. Fix macaroni & cheese as directed.
2. Brown ground beef and drain.
3. Combine beef, prepared macaroni and chili seasoning, stirring until well mixed. Serves 6.

Patrick Linbeck   **University of Notre Dame**

Impossible Cheeseburger Pie

1 lb. ground beef
1 c. chopped onion
1½ c. milk
3 eggs

¾ c. Bisquick
¼ t. pepper
2 tomatoes
1 c. shredded cheddar cheese

Heat oven to 400°. Grease pie plate with butter or oil. Brown beef and onion, drain. Spread on plate. Beat milk, eggs, Bisquick, salt and pepper in blender for 15 seconds. Pour over meat. Bake 25 minutes. Top with sliced tomatoes and cheese. Bake about 8 more minutes. Serves 6.

Catherine Young   **University of Houston**

Beef Stroganoff

1. Have butcher cut 2 pounds of round steak into thin strips.
2. Put meat in paper bag with seasoned flour. Shake to coat meat.
3. Brown meat in oil.
4. Add 1 chopped onion and 1 can (4 oz.) of mushrooms -brown.
5. Add 1 can of beef consomme soup, ¾ can of tomato soup, ⅓ can of white wine and dash of Worcestershire sauce.
6. Cover and cook in electric skillet at 250° for 1 hour.
7. Before serving, mix in 1 pint of sour cream.
8. Serve over rice or noodles. Serves 6.

W. Scott Locher   **Stanford University**

Cheesey Beef Pie

1 lb. ground beef
½ c. chopped onion
⅛ oz. can tomato sauce
¼ c. snipped parsley
¼ t. dried oregano leaves, crushed

1 3 oz. can chopped mushrooms, drained
2 pkgs. refrigerated crescent rolls (8 rolls each)
3 eggs
6 slices sharp American cheese

Brown beef and onion, drain. Mix next 4 ingredients and ⅛ t. pepper with beef. Open one package rolls. Place 4 sections of dough together forming 12 x 6 rectangle. Seal edges and perforations and roll to a 12" square, then fit into a 9" pie plate and trim. Separate one of the eggs - set yolk aside. Beat egg white with remaining 2 eggs. Spread ½ over dough. Spoon meat into shell. Arrange cheese slices over the meat. Spread rest of egg mixture over cheese. Rollout second package of rolls as before. Place on top of filling. Trim and flute edge. Cut slits for steam. Brush top with yolk mixture. Bake at 350° for 50-55 minutes. If pastry gets too brown, cover with foil. Let stand 10 minutes. Serves 6.

Kimberly Hawsey   **Baylor University**

5-Spice Beef Casserole

1 lb. ground beef
1 T. olive oil
½ onion, chopped
⅛ t. garlic powder
⅛ t. thyme
⅛ t. oregano

1 bay leaf
1 can tomatoes (16 oz.)
1 can cream of mushroom soup
1 c. cooked Minute Rice
1 c. grated cheddar cheese

Brown meat in oil, add onions. Cook until tender. Stir in remaining ingredients except cheese. Bring to boil; reduce heat and simmer 5 minutes. Pour into casserole dish and top with cheese. Bake at 350° for 30 minutes. Serves 6.

Mindy Lobliner   **University of Houston**

Beef Stroganoff

1 box Hamburger Helper
Beef and Noodle Mix

1½ lbs. ground beef, cooked
1 pt. sour cream

Mix according to package directions. *Just before serving* add sour cream and heat slowly. If heat is too high, the sour cream will separate, so watch carefully. Serves 6.

Lisa Platt　　　　　　　　　　　　**University of Arizona**

Red Raider Stroganoff

1½ lb. round steak (lean)
1 can Campbell's Cream of
Mushroom Soup
4 oz. mushrooms, fresh

1 whole white onion
8 oz. sour cream
1 T. pepper
1 pkg. noodles

Cut steak into thin strips - simmer it in electric skillet with mushrooms (fresh) and onions and pepper for 30 minutes. Then add mushroom soup; sour cream. Simmer for 15 more minutes. Serve on bed of noodles. Delicious! Serves 4-6. "Go Tech"

Tony Jolann　　　　　　　　　　　**Texas Tech University**

No Peek Casserole

2 lbs. stewing beef, cut into
1 inch cubes
1 envelope onion soup mix
1 10¾ oz. can condensed
cream of mushroom soup

1 4 oz. can whole mushrooms,
drained
½ c. red wine

Combine ingredients in a 2-quart casserole. Cover. Bake at 300° for 3 hours. Don't peek until almost done. Serve over rice or noodles. Serves 6.

Martha Harrington　　　　　　　　**Stanford University**

James' Chili Pie

Fritos or Doritos   **Chili**
Cheese - Velveeta or rat

Put chips in bowl. Heat chili real hot. Pour over chips. Top with grated cheese. Add chopped onions if desired. Serves 4 - 6.

James Reckling   **Ole Miss**

Super Steak

The easiest way ever to sauce up a steak in no time at all.

Lea & Perrins   **Soy sauce**
   Worcestershire Sauce   **Garlic powder**

First poke the steak with a fork several times, so that the seasoning will seep in. Splash Worcestershire sauce and soy sauce until steak is covered and then sprinkle with garlic powder. Let set for at least ½ an hour before cooking on the grill.

Susan Henslet   **Baylor University**

Beef Tips

2 lbs. kabob meat or sirloin   **1 envelope onion soup mix**
2 cans mushroom soup   **1 10½ oz. can whole**
1 can water or ½ c. red wine   **mushrooms, drained**

Cut meat into small pieces. To meat add mushroom soup, onion soup mix, mushrooms, and wine *or* water. Bake covered at 300° for 3 hours. Serves 6.

Patrick Linbeck   **University of Notre Dame**

Flank Steak

¼ c. soy sauce
3 T. honey
2 T. vinegar
1½ t. garlic powder
1½ t. ground ginger

¾ c. oil
1 c. chopped onion
1½ pounds flank steak
Optional mushrooms - they
   add great flavor

Stir all of the above together. Pour over steak. Marinate overnight. Cook on grill 7 minutes each side. Serves 4-6.

Sheryl Durkee   **Ole Miss**

Roast Beef Tender

Rub a large beef tender, about 3-4 lbs. with a mixture of:
Kitchen Bouquet, olive oil, garlic salt and Lawry Seasoned Salt.

Let meat sit for at least one hour. Preheat oven to 475°. Cook for 45 minutes for medium rare, add 5 minutes a lb. for medium. Test roast by cutting into it. Serves 6-8.

Susan Miller   **Baylor University**

Fettuccine

8 oz. fettuccine noodles
1 T. butter
½ pt. whipping cream
2 T. dried parsley (fresh
   if available)

¼ c. grated Parmesan cheese
Salt and pepper to taste

Boil noodles, follow directions on box. Drain. Add butter, cream, and cheese. If too creamy, add more cheese. Add parsley. Salt and pepper. For an extra touch add marinated mushrooms or steamed broccoli. Serves 4-6. Serve immediately.

Hope Bradberry   **University of Tulsa**

Fettuccine

1 bag fettuccine noodles
1 can Parmesan cheese
1 pt. whipping cream
1 egg

1 8 oz. sour cream
  (use to your taste)
¼ stick butter
Salt and pepper to taste

Boil noodles the desired time until they are soft. Drain all excess water. In a bowl, put noodles then Parmesan cheese, butter, sour cream, whipping cream, egg and salt and pepper to taste. Stir all of the ingredients together until it is creamy texture. Serve immediately. Serves 4-6.

Lisa Franklin   **University of Mississippi**

Macho Fettucine

1 lb. Italian sausage
1 can cream chicken soup

2 c. sour cream
1 pkg. fresh frozen fettucine

Cook fettucine and drain. Cut up Italian sausage into small pieces. Brown sausage over medium high heat for about 8 minutes. Place on paper towel to drain grease. Mix all ingredients together. Put into a 6" x 18" Pyrex dish. Bake 30 minutes at 350°. Serves 4-6.

Richard Duffy   **University of Arkansas**

Fettuccine

1 box (Prince) folded
  fettuccine
1 c. heavy cream
1 stick butter

6 oz. Parmesan cheese
Salt, pepper to taste

Boil water, add fettuccine and cook through. In separate pan, melt butter. Add cream slowly and stir. Add parmesan cheese, salt and pepper. Toss sauce with cooked fettuccine. Serves 4-6.

Elizabeth A. Wall   **Dartmouth College**

Irish Italian Spaghetti

1 chopped onion
2 T. oil (salad or olive)
1 lb. ground beef
1 t. salt
½ t. chili powder
½ t. Tabasco
¼ t. black pepper
Dash red pepper
1 can cream of mushroom
  soup
1 can tomato soup
1 8 oz. pkg. long spaghetti
½ c. grated Parmesan cheese

Cook onion in hot oil until golden. Add meat and seasonings. Brown lightly. Cover, simmer 10 minutes. Pour off excess oil, if any. Add soups, cover and simmer 45 minutes. Cook spaghetti in boiling salted water until tender. Drain and rinse with hot water. Arrange on hot platter. Pour sauce over spaghetti. Sprinkle with cheese. Serves 4-6.

Janet Gage   **Southern Methodist University**

Spaghetti

2 large jars Prego spaghetti
  sauce with mushrooms
1 lb. ground beef, cooked
1 c. grated cheddar cheese
8 oz. cooked spaghetti

Combine all ingredients and heat. Serve with green salad with creamy Italian dressing and buttered sliced French bread. (Heat bread in oven while cooking spaghetti sauce.) Serves 4-6.

Lisa Platt   **University of Arizona**

Pepperoni Pizza Casserole

6 oz. macaroni noodles
8 oz. spaghetti sauce
4 oz. mozzarella cheese,
  shredded
8 oz. cottage cheese
4 oz. sliced pepperoni
½ c. onions, chopped

Cook macaroni and drain. In large casserole, combine all ingredients and blend. Sprinkle Parmeasan cheese on top if desired. Cover and bake for 30 minutes in oven 350°. Serves 4-6.

Vanessa Rothstein   **Georgetown University**

Lasagna Casserole

2 T. salad oil
2 garlic cloves, crushed
1 lb. hamburger, crumbled
1 8 oz. can tomato sauce
1 #2 can tomatoes
Pepper

½ t. oregano
8 oz. lasagna noodles
½ lb. sliced mozzarella cheese
¾ lb. ricotta or cottage cheese

Saute hamburger and garlic in oil. Add the next 4 ingredients and simmer 20 minutes. While it simmers, cook noodles in boiling water about 15 minutes and drain. Fill a big buttered casserole with alternate layers of noodles, cheese, tomato, meat, sauce and Parmesan, ending with a layer of sauce and Parmesan. Bake at 375° for 20 minutes uncovered. Serves 6.

Nancy Kepner   Baylor University

Laster Lasagne

1 can tomato puree
2 cans tomato paste
1½ c. water
2 t. oregano
1 t. salt
1 t. pepper
1 t. olive oil
2 c. minced onion

1 clove garlic, minced into
   tiny pieces
1½ lbs. ground beef
1 t. salt
1 lb. lasagne noodles
1 lb. mozzarella cheese
1 lb. ricotta cheese
4 oz. Romano cheese

Simmer in a large pot the tomato puree and paste, water, oregano, salt and pepper. Sautc in a skillet the olive oil, meat, onion, garlic and salt until meat is brown. Add meat to large pot. Simmer for 2 hours. Add ¼ c. of good cooking brandy. Layer in a large pan, first the noodles, then cheese and sauce and repeat finishing with noodles and sauce on top. Bake at 375° for 30-45 minutes. Serves 6-8.

N. Scott Laster   Texas Tech University

Grilled Shrimp Shish-Ka-Bobs

Not a quick dish, but great for a group of about 6 good friends on Friday or Saturday night or after Yale beats Harvard anytime!

Need:

About 36 big peeled shrimp	Stick of butter
Lots of mushrooms	A couple of lemons
Pineapple	Lots of beer or
Bacon	margaritas
Peppers	
Onions	

Peel the shrimp. Have a beer. Wash all the vegetables. Have a beer. Melt butter and squeeze lemon. Have a beer. Put everything on skewers, making sure shrimp has bacon on both sides. Have yet another. Cook on open grill until the shrimp looks pink. Serve and of course, enjoy. Can't talk about politics or academics during dinner. Recommended music: Jimmy Buffet. Serves 6.

David Randall   **Yale University**

Shrimp Minali

5 lbs. shrimp in shell	½ t. cayenne pepper
2 sticks butter	2 cloves garlic, minced
5-6 oz. olive oil	or powdered
2 T. cracked pepper	1½ bay leaf
2 T. rosemary	Salt to taste

Bake shrimp in mixture ½ to ¾ hour at 350°, be sure shrimp is in a single layer. Squeeze 2 lemons over shrimp after cooking. Serve with salad, french bread, beer or wine. Serves 6-8.

Jane Spooner   **Baylor University**

Boiled Shrimp

Peel and clean shrimp. Cover with cold water. Add salt, 1 T. lemon juice and 2 bay leaves for each lb. of shrimp. Put shrimp into water. Bring to *rolling* boil. Remove immediately from stove. Rinse under cold water. Then put in pan of salted ice water until cold. Drain and refrigerate. 1 lb. serves 3 people.

Tom Johnson   Stanford University

Crab and Shrimp with Almonds

1 generous c. lump crab
1 generous c. shrimp (cooked)
1 c. finely chopped celery
¼ c. minced green onion

1 can Chinese dried noodles
1 c. slivered almonds, sauteed
   in butter for 3 minutes.
¼ t. salt
¼ t. pepper
2 T. Worcestershire sauce

Mix all ingredients and place in a greased casserole and refrigerate. When ready to serve mix in half of the Chinese fixed noodles and toasted slivered almonds. Season with salt, pepper, Worcestershire sauce; top with Chinese noodles and bake uncovered 20-25 minutes at 350°. Serves 6.

Ronnie Jacobe   Princeton University

Creamy Chicken

1 2½ oz. jar sliced dried beef
4 boneless chicken breasts
2 cans cream of mushroom
   soup

1 c. sour cream
6 slices bacon - cut in half

In a shallow baking dish arrange single layer of beef and top with 8 pieces of chicken. Blend soup and sour cream and pour over all. Top with bacon. Cover and bake at 250° for 4 hours. Uncover, stir sauce and bake uncovered for 1 hour more. Serve with plain rice or curried rice. Serves 4.

Mancha White   Randolph-Macon Woman's College

Baked Chicken and Sour Cream

3 lbs. chicken parts
6 slices of bacon
1 c. sour cream
8 oz. marcaroni

1 10½ oz. can condensed
   cream of mushroom soup
Minced parsley

At 350°, bake chicken and bacon slices for 45 minutes. Blend soup and sour cream; pour over chicken; bake for 30 minutes. Cook macaroni. Place chicken in a dish. Mix macaroni with mushroom sour cream sauce, which is remaining in pan from cooked chicken. Garnish with parsley. Serves 4.

Glenn Klimchuk   **Brown University**

Chicken Broccoli Casserole

2½ c. diced cooked chicken
1 pkg. broccoli spears
   (thawed)
1 can chicken mushroom
   soup

2 T. lemon juice
½ c. Hellmans mayonnaise
¼ c. milk
½ pkg. Stove Top Dressing

Put chicken on bottom of casserole. Arrange broccoli on top. Mix other ingredients and pour or spread over. Before baking, sprinkle dressing over top and drizzle with melted butter. Bake at 375° for ½ hour or until bubbly. Serves 4.

Page Mason   **Texas Christian University**

Chicken Casserole

3 boned chicken breasts
1 pkg. bacon (6 strips)
1 pkg. Budding Corned Beef

1 can cream of mushroom
   soup
8 oz. carton of sour cream
1 small can of mushrooms
   (optional)

Line the bottom of an 8″ square casserole dish with the corned beef slices. Separate chicken breasts into 6 parts. Wrap beasts with a strip of bacon and place in casserole dish. Sprinkle with seasoning if desired. Mix sour cream with mushroom soup and pour over the top. 1 can (small) of mushrooms can be added. Bake for 1 hour at 325°. Serves 6.

Kathy Boles   **University of Texas at Austin**

Easy Chicken Salad

2 chicken breasts without
  the bone
¼ c. mayonnaise

1 T. lemon juice
Salt & pepper

Bake chicken breasts at 350° for 30 minutes. Cool. Remove skin and cut into small pieces. Mix with the remaining ingredients. Serve on lettuce or cut open a croissant and stuff it with chicken salad. Serves 4.

John McCracken   Old Dominion University

Chicken Casserole

12 hard tortillas cut into
  bite size or Doritos
2 cans cream of chicken soup
1 soup can of milk
1 can Oretga Chiles, chopped

4 chicken breasts, cooked
  and cut into bite size pieces
Salt to taste
8 oz. sharp cheddar cheese,
  grated

Put above ingredients in layers. Make the day before and refrigerate for 24 hours. Bake at 350° until hot. Serves 4-6

Ronnie Jacobe   Princeton University

Chicken Curry

2½-3 lb. chicken
1 rib of celery, diced
  very fine
½ medium onion, diced
2 T. butter or margarine

2 cans cream of chicken soup
1 can cream of celery soup
½ c. chicken broth
3-4 t. Spice Island curry
  powder, to taste

Cook and bone chicken in water 1 hour, cut into pieces. Saute rib of celery and onion in 2 T. of butter or margarine in a double boiler. When melted, add soup. Thin with chicken broth. Season to taste with curry powder. Add chicken, let blend, serve over rice. Condiments: chopped peanuts, chopped green onions, currents, bananas, crushed pineapples, white grapes, hard-boiled eggs, chutney and coconut. Serves 4-6.

Peter Stinner   Trinity University

Chicken Breasts and Rice Casserole

6 slices bacon
1 c. Uncle Ben's Rice
4-6 chicken breasts
1 pinch garlic salt
1 can cream of chicken soup

1 t. oregano
1 t. dried parsley
Paprika
Nutmeg

Line oblong (8½ x 11″) Pyrex baking casserole with raw bacon. Sprinkle rice over bacon. Salt, pepper and paprika the chicken breasts and place on top of rice. Thin the chicken soup with 1 can of water and pour over all. Sprinkle garlic salt, pinch of nutmeg, oregano and parlsey over top of all. Cover dish with *heavy* foil and bake at 300° for 2 hours without peeking! Serves 4.

Ronnie Jacobe   **Princeton University**

Chicken Breast with Lemon & Brandy

6 whole chicken breasts,
    split, skinned, boned
½ c. flour
1 t. oregano
Salt & pepper to taste

½ c. lemon juice
½ c. brandy
2 T. parsley, finely chopped

Mix flour and oregano. Dredge chicken in flour mixture. Saute chicken in hot butter, turning and seasoning, about 12 minutes or till white and tender. Add lemon juice and brandy. Set brandy on fire. When the flame is out, garnish with parsley. Serve over rice, spooning extra sauce over chicken.

Cooking Hint: Poultry may be stuffed the night before roasting, if both the bird and the stuffing are first well chilled.

Stefanie White   **Baylor University**

Bar-B-Que Chicken-A-La-Randall

Strictly a beer and country music dinner. Preferably Lone Star and Hank Williams, Jr. Willie Nelson will always suffice in a jam.

2 chickens, cut up
Jalapenos
Hot bar-b-que sauce from
  store
Worcestershire sauce
Salt and pepper

Another Friday or Saturday night dinner 'cause it takes some time. Anyway, salt and pepper chicken. Mix everything else in bowl for sauce, throw in some beer; the amount depending upon the current state of inebriation. Cook the chickens on the grill for 30 minutes with the meaty side up. Then ten minutes on the flip side. Don't forget to put the sauce on it and "put a cold one in your hand" as Hank Jr. says. Serves 4.

David Randall   **Yale University**

Easy Chicken Little

4-6 boneless chicken breasts
  cut in half
Stick of margarine or butter
Progresso Italian bread
  crumbs
Salt and pepper
Grated Parmesan cheese
  (optional)

Dip each chicken piece in butter and then roll in bread crumbs to coat. Place on large cookie sheet and add, salt, pepper and sprinkle with cheese to taste. Bake 350° for 45 minutes to 1 hour. (Other small pieces of chicken may be substituted for chicken breasts.) Serves 6.

Susan Gaetz   **Vanderbilt University**

Chicken D'Lite

2 breasts of chicken
Garlic salt (to taste)

Lemon pepper (to taste)
Dash of salt and pepper

Bake chicken in oven heated to 375° for 30 minutes. Sprinkle items on chicken prior to cooking. Serves 2.

Susannah Moore   **University of Florida**

Chicken A La Troy

8 thighs or 8 legs of chicken
1 medium onion

1 stick of real butter
3 c. sliced mushrooms

In a large saucepan melt butter. Put sliced onion and mushrooms in butter. Heat on warm. Remove skin from chicken and place chicken in the large saucepan. Make only one layer deep. Cook for 1½ hours on medium heat. Occasionally turn chicken over to prevent burning the bottom. Serves 8.

Shannon Burton   **University of Southern California**

Chicken Divan (usually double)

4 large chicken breasts
1 T. butter to grease casserole
2 pkgs. broccoli, frozen
2 cans cream of chicken soup

1 c. mayonnaise
1 t. lemon
1 t. curry powder
Bread crumbs for top of
    casserole

Wash chicken in cold water. Put in pot and cover with water to top breasts. Add celery tops and slices of onion. Bring to a boil; boil for about 45 minutes to 1 hour. Remove chicken. Boil broccoli in same liquid according to directions. Drain broccoli and discard liquid. In same pan, mix soup, mayo, lemon and curry.

Skin and bone chicken. In a casserole dish, layer broccoli, chunks of chicken, and soup mixture. Top with bread crumbs. Bake for 45 minutes at 350° degrees. Serves 4.

Eve Mueller   **Southern Methodist University**

Baked Chicken, Italian Style

Chicken pieces
Progresso bread crumbs
½ c. butter, melted
Salt and pepper

Season chicken pieces with salt and pepper. Roll in melted butter, then roll in bread crumbs. Place on foil on cookie sheet and bake at 375° for 1 hour.

John Walton   University of Houston

Chicken Casserole

2-3 lb. chicken
1 large onion, chopped fine
½ c. canned mushrooms
1 c. chopped celery
½ c. chopped black olives
½ c. almonds
1 box cooked Rice-A-Roni
   (chicken or almond fried)

Boil chicken in water until done, about 1 hour, save the broth. Cut chicken into small pieces. Mix all remaining ingredients except almonds & olives. Add enough broth so mixture will not be dried. Put in a large casserole dish and top with olives and almonds. Bake at 325° for 30-35 minutes.

Suzanne Jablonowski   Texas Tech University

Chicken Casserole

4 c. cooked chunks chicken
   (3 lb. chicken)
2 c. coarsely chopped celery
   (6-8 stalks)
2 c. Pepperidge Farm
   cornbread stuffing
1 c. Hellman's mayonnaise
½ c. milk
¼ c. chopped onions
8 oz. pkg. Swiss cheese slices
   julienned
1 t. salt
Dash pepper
½ c. slivered almonds

Mix all ingredients. Put in 9 x 13 pan. Bake covered 350° oven 30-40 minutes. Bake 10 minutes more uncovered. Serves 4.

Lynn Drury   Texas Christian University

Chicken and Almonds

2 whole chicken breasts (boned and cut into thin strips)
1 c. almonds
¼ c. salad oil
1 c. onion slices (green onions with tops)
1½ c. cut celery sliced on an angle
1¼ c. chicken broth
1-2 carrots cut cross-wise (circles)
1 can mushrooms - 4 oz. (can use fresh ones)
3 T. green peas (frozen looks best)
1 t. sugar
1 T. cornstarch
¼ c. soy sauce
2 T. cooking sherry
1 5 oz. can bamboo shoots, drained
1 5 oz. can sliced water chestnuts, drained

1. In skillet toast almonds in oil; stir constantly; drain on paper towel.
2. Put chicken in same skillet; sprinkle with salt; stir 5-10 minutes until tender (can cut with wooden spoon). Remove chicken.
3. Add onions, celery, carrots, mushrooms (if fresh), and ½ c. chicken broth. Cook uncovered 5 minutes or until vegetables are slightly tender.
4. Combine sugar, cornstarch, soy sauce, cooking sherry to make a paste. Add this paste to the above. Add remaining broth. Cook and stir until it thickens. (Won't be really thick, but far from watery.)
5. Add chicken, bamboo shoots, water chestnuts, mushrooms (if canned), peas and all but ½ c. almonds. (I usually just dump in all almonds now.)
6. Heat thoroughly.

Serve over rice. (Cook rice in chicken broth for extra flavor.) Serve with Chinese snow peas. Serves 4-6.

Cathryn George   **Southern Methodist University**

Aunt Donna's Chicken Supreme

8 boneless chicken breasts
¾ c. mayonnaise
1 can cream of mushroom
  soup
1 can cream of chicken soup
1 c. grated cheddar cheese
2-3 c. dry stuffing mix
  (Pepperidge Farm)

Cut chicken into small pieces. Cover bottom of pan with chicken, mix soups and mayonnaise. Spread evenly over chicken. Sprinkle cheese over creamy mixture. Cover with stuffing. Cook in preheated 350° oven for ½ hour covered and ½ hour uncovered. Serve HOT! Serves 6-8 people.

Susan J. Lindemann   **University of Virginia**

Cashew Chicken

3 boned chicken breasts
½ lb. snow peas
½ lb. mushrooms
4 green onions
½ t. salt
¼ c. peanut oil
4 oz. cashews

SAUCE MIX:
1 c. chicken stock
¼ c. soy sauce
2 T. cornstarch
½ t. sugar

Remove skins from chicken. Slice into small pieces. Slice mushrooms and onions. Heat oil and stir fry cashews. Remove. Stir fry chicken until it is opaque. Add onions and stir fry a minute. Add mushrooms and snow peas. Stir fry 2 minutes. add cashews. Add sauce mix. Stir well and serve with rice. Serves 6.

Patrick Linbeck   **University of Notre Dame**

Scrumptious Chicken Salad

1 whole chicken
½ c. mayonnaise
¾ c. Ranch dressing
½ c. almonds (roasted)

1-2 c. grapes
½ c. chopped celery
Cavendirs seasoning (or
  any other salt-seasoning)

Boil chicken. Strip off meat and tear into bite size pieces. Put into large bowl. Mix with mayonniase, ranch dressing, grapes, and celery. Sprinkle seasoning on top and stir in. Refrigerate. Mix roasted almonds in when ready to serve. Great alone, on sandwiches or on crackers. Serves 4.

Catherine Anne Couch   **University of Virginia**

Chicken in Red Wine Sauce

3 or 4 lbs. chicken pieces,
  salt and peppered
1 c. any kind dry, red wine

¼ c. Tamarin soy sauce
2-3 cloves garlic, chopped

Place all the above in covered casserole. Bake at 375° for 1 hour, then ½ hour uncovered. Serve over rice. Serves 4.

Heidi Sparks   **Syracuse University**

Chicken/Rice Casserole

1 whole chicken
2 c. white rice

1 can cream of chicken soup

In a large pot, cover chicken with cold water, add salt, 1 carrot, 1 onion, 1 stalk of celery and boil for at least 45 minutes. Bone chicken and set aside. Cook the rice 20 minutes in 4 cups of the chicken broth after discarding the veggies. Mix the cream of chicken soup with a can of the remaining broth. In a casserole, layer the rice, boned chicken and soup mixture. Bake at 350° for 50 minutes. Chicken breasts can be substituted for the whole chicken, they aren't as messy. Serves 4.

Nina Taylor   **Texas A&M University**

Oven Fried Chicken

2 chicken breasts (cut
  in half)

1 cup Kellogs Corn Flakes
  crumbs
½ c. milk

Dip chicken in milk. Roll in the corn flakes crumbs. Bake 350° 45 minutes - 1 hour. Serves 2.

Elizabeth Martin   **University of Oklahoma**

Chicken Enchiladas

24 flour tortillas
4½ to 5 lbs. boiled chicken
  (save broth)
2 cans green chiles, chopped
2 pints sour cream

1 large onion, chopped,
  sauteed in butter
1 pkg. chopped frozen
  spinach, cooked & drained
1 lb. Monterey Jack cheese,
  grated

Mix above together (except tortillas and cheese). Dip tortillas in broth. Line center of tortilla with tablespoon or so of mixture. Roll up tortillas. Line oblong casserole dish with enchiladas. Cover with cheese and remaining sauce. Bake at 350° for 20-30 minutes.

Marie Ungerbuehler   **Baylor University**

Chicken Enchiladas

20 flour or corn tortillas
Cream filling (at right)
2/3 c. whipping cream
2 c. Monterey Jack and
  cheddar cheese mixed

Cream Filling:
2 c. sour cream
1 c. chopped green onions,
  some tops
¼ t. cumin
3 c. cheddar cheese, grated
1 chicken, cooked and diced
  or 4 large cooked chicken
  breasts, diced

Mix sour cream, cumin, cheddar cheese and cut up chicken. Fry tortillas until soft or place about 4 wrapped in a towel put in microwave for 45 seconds to 1 minute. Place mixture in soft tortillas, roll and place seam side down in casserole. Moisten top of enchiladas with whipping cream and sprinkle with Monterey Jack and cheddar cheese. Bake at 375° for 20 minutes. Serves 8.

Amanda Justice   **Randolph-Macon Woman's College**

Quick Green Enchiladas

2 lbs. ground beef
½ c. chopped onion
½ c. shredded cheddar cheese
12 flour tortillas

2 cans cream of chicken soup
2 (4 oz.) cans chopped green chiles
2 (5.3 oz. cans) evaporated milk
1 lb. Velveeta cheese, chunks

Brown and drain fat from ground beef. Add onion and cheddar cheese. Divide mixture among 12 tortillas, roll up and put in 13x9x2 baking pan. For sauce, heat soup, chiles, milk and cheese until melted. Be careful not to burn. Pour over enchiladas. Bake 20 minutes at 400°. Serves 4-6.

W. Scott Locher   Stanford University

Pilati's Fajitas

2¼ lb. skirt steak
¼ c. pineapple juice
¼ c. orange juice
¼ c. white wine
¼ c. lemon juice
¾ c. water

¼ c. soy sauce
1 T. pepper
1 clove garlic
3 dried chiles arboles
3 T. butter
Rind of one orange & lemon

Place meat in glass dish. Combine remaining ingredients and pour over meat. Marinate for no more than 2 hours, grill over hot fire, basting with marinade. Makes 4-6 servings. YUM!

John Pilati   University of Texas at Austin

Allen's Fajitas

2½ lb. fajita meat or
  flank steak
1 can beer
1 can Rotel tomatoes
  and chiles

2 T. fajitas seasoning
Lime juice: 2 limes
Worcestershire sauce

Season meat with fajita seasoning. Take a plastic garbage bag and place meat in it. Add beer, Rotel tomatoes, chiles, lime juice and Worcestershire sauce. Close bag and marinate meat *overnight* in the ice box.

Grill over hot coals close to the fire 4 minutes each side. Serve with flour tortillas and hot sauce. Serves 6.

Allen Crosswell   Ole Miss

Green Chili Quiche

6 eggs	1 t. salt
1 lb. Monterrey Jack Cheese	1 can (4 oz.) chopped green
1 frozen deep pan pie shell	chiles

Mix eggs, chiles and salt together, pour into the pie shell. Grate cheese and layer on top. Bake at 375° for 45 minutes. Allow 10 minutes to cool before serving. Serves 6.

J.C. Taylor   **Texas A&M University**

Andrew's Fajitas

5 lbs. tenderized fajita meat	4 sliced jalapeno peppers
(flank steak)	1 t. salt
1 bottle Kraft Italian	1 t. pepper
dressing	1 beer
1 bottle Worcestershire sauce	½ onion, chopped
2 lemons	½ garlic clove, chopped
2 tomatoes	
1 stick of butter	

Mix all ingredients (except meat) into a sauce. Bring the sauce to a boil. Let cool and add meat. Let the meat sit in the sauce (an Igloo cooler is recommended) anywhere from 1 hour to 2 days. Remove meat and charcoal over hot fire. Serve meat with tortillas. It is recommended to add picante sauce, sour cream, and cheese. Serves 8.

Patrick Linbeck   **University of Notre Dame**

Chalupas

3 to 4 lbs. pork roast	2 t. cumin seed
1 lb. pinto beans	1 t. oregano
2 cloves garlic	1 t. Tabasco
2 T. chili powder	Salt to taste

Place roast in large roaster. Add water to cover roast. Add rest of ingredients. Cook, covered at least 8 hours over low heat, stirring occasionally. Let cool, remove bone and shred meat. Build chalupas in the following order: crushed tortilla chips, meat and bean mixture, chopped lettuce, chopped avocados, chopped onion, grated cheese, sour cream and picante sauce.

Katie Dupuy   **Baylor University**

Mexican Salad Bar

Place on buffet in this order:

1. **Fritos (regular) 2 bags**
2. **Chiles, use the canned green ones**
3. **Beans, any kind you like**
4. **Cheese, 1 lb. Monterrey Jack and cheddar cheese, shredded**
5. **Sour Cream - 16 oz.**
6. **Shredded lettuce - 1 head**
7. **Cut up tomatoes - 3 large**
8. **Cut up black olives - 2 cups**
9. **Avocados - 6 (mashed, salted, lemon juice)**
10. **Mexican style red chili sauce - 2 10 oz. cans**
11. **Purple onions chopped - 3 large**
12. **Chopped bell peppers - 2**

First put chips on the plate, then pile on whatever you like. Ole! Serves 20.

Denise DeCell   **Texas Tech University**

Chalupas

2 to 3 lb. pork roast	Crushed chips (Tostitos)
1 lb. pinto beans	Shredded lettuce
2 cloves garlic	Diced tomatoes
2 T. chili powder	Chopped avocados
2 t. cumin seed	Chopped onions
1 t. oregano	Grated cheese
1 t. Tabasco	Sour cream
Salt to taste	Picante sauce

Place roast in large roaster and cover with water. Add rest of seasonings and beans. Cook covered for at least 8 hours over low heat, stirring occasionally. Remove bone and shred the meat. Build chalupas in following order:

1. Crushed Tostitos or Dorito chips
2. Meat and bean mixture
3. Shredded lettuce
4. Diced tomatoes

Etc. . . build as you desire!! Serves a lot!

Laura Boughton   **Ole Miss**

Tex-Mex Dinner

3 medium avocados
Salt and pepper to taste
½ c. mayonnaise
2 cans (10½ oz.) bean dip
3 medium tomatoes, coarsely
  chopped
2 3½ oz. cans ripe olives
Round tortillas

2 T. lemon juice
8 oz. sour cream
1 pkg. taco seasoning mix
1 bunch of onions,
  chopped (1 cup)
16 oz. sharp cheddar cheese,
  shredded

Peel, pit and mash avocados. Add lemon juice, salt and pepper. Combine sour cream, mayonnaise and taco seasoning mix. Spread the 2 cans of bean dip on a large shallow serving platter. Top with the avocado mixture. Over the avocado mixture, spread the sour cream and taco seasoning mixture. Sprinkle with the onions and tomatoes and olives, then cover with the cheese. Serve with the tortilla chips. Note: Browned hamburger meat can be added on top of the bean dip. Serves 4.

Angela Johnson   **Baylor University**

Mexican Chicken

1 large fryer
1 pkg. tortillas
1 medium onion, chopped
1 medium green bell pepper,
  chopped
1 T. margarine
1 lb. mild cheddar cheese
1¼ t. chili powder

½ t. garlic salt
1 can cream of chicken soup
1 can cream of mushroom
  soup
1 lb. can stewed tomatoes
Few drops Tabasco

Boil chicken in slightly salted water until tender. Let cool and bone. Cut into 1 inch pieces. Save chicken broth and let cool. Place tortillas in broth for 15 minutes. In pan, layer tortillas first, then chicken pieces. Saute onion and bell pepper in margarine and sprinkle over chicken. Next sprinkle ½ lb. grated cheese over, then chili powder and garlic salt. Spread on soups and then another layer of tortillas. Mix tomatoes and Tabasco. Spread over top. Sprinkle remaining cheese on top. Bake at 375° for 30 minutes until hot and bubbly. They'll think you're a gourmet! Proven effective! Serves 4-6.

Kay McCullough   **Baylor University**

Pocket Sandwiches

1 c. chopped cooked chicken
  or beef
1 c. frozen, chopped broccoli,
  cooked and drained
½ c. chopped tomatoes
1 hard-boiled egg, chopped

2 oz. (½ c.) shredded
  mozzarella cheese
½ c. mayonnaise
1 T. Dijon mustard
4 (Pita) pocket breads, halved

Combine chicken or beef, broccoli, avocado, tomatoes, cheese and egg in a bowl. In another bowl, combine mayonnaise and mustard and pour over mixture, tossing to coat. Spoon approximately ½ cup mixture into each pocket half. Serves 4.

Cindy Kaczmarek   Georgetown University

Hot Curried Fruit

1 large can pear halves,
  cut up
1 large can peach halves,
  cut up
1 large jar of Maraschino
  cherries (Mandarin oranges
  are optional)

¼ c. dark brown sugar
2 T. curry powder
¼ c. brandy

Mix ingredients. Place in a casserole dish. Put in refrigerator overnight. Take out and let come to room temperature. Bake at 350° for about 30 minutes or until hot throughout. Serves 6-8.

James Giles   University of Texas at Austin

Vegetable Salad

2 c. raw cauliflower, chopped
2 c. raw broccoli, chopped
1 10 oz. pkg. frozen peas
¼ c. chopped green onion
1 c. celery, chopped
¼ c. chopped green pepper

Mix together:
¼ c. mayonnaise
½ pint sour cream
1 envelope Hidden Valley
  Original Ranch Dressing

Toss vegetables with the dressing. Serves 8-10.

Stephanie Moore   Oakland University

Mexican Tortilla Breakfast

2 tortillas
2 slices of cheese

2 eggs
Picante sauce

Melt cheese on tortilla in microwave while frying the egg. Place fried egg on cheese tortilla and top with picante sauce. Serves 2.

Optional: Sauteed mushrooms and onions on top also.

Bruce Collins   **Southern Methodist University**

Tuna Salad

1 6½ oz. can tuna
¼ c. mayonnaise
¼ c. black olives (chopped)
¼ c. chopped boiled eggs

¼ c. chopped pickles
Mustard (to taste)
Pepper (to taste)

Mix ingredients well. Refrigerate for 30 minutes. Serve on crackers, for sandwiches, or just alone. Serves 2.

Ana Kirk   **Trinity University**

Stuffed Potatoes

4 large potatoes
5 T. butter or margarine
2 eggs

6 oz. shredded American or
  cheddar cheese
6 oz. diced cooked ham

Bake potatoes at 375° for about 1 hour or until done. Cut potatoes in half lengthwise and scoop out insides, leaving skins. In a large bowl, beat potatoes 1 minute, add margarine, eggs and salt and pepper as desired and beat until smooth. Fold in half the cheese and all the ham. Fill the skins with the mixture, top with remaining cheese and place on cookie sheet. Bake for 15-20 minutes or until potatoes are heated and cheese is melted. Makes 8 servings.

Lisa Conomy   **Georgetown University**

Spinach Salad (with Mushrooms)

8 c. fresh spinach leaves
4 oz. fresh mushrooms, sliced
¼ t. salt
¼ t. garlic salt

3 T. red wine vinegar
¼ c. oil
Parmesan cheese
Pepper

In bowl, combine mushrooms, salts, pepper, oil and vinegar. Place spinach leaves in separate bowl, and then add combined mixture. Toss, and sprinkle with Parmesan cheese. Serves 8.

Stephen Watkins   Georgetown University

No Toss Salad

1 large head lettuce
1 or 2 pkgs. frozen peas
2 c. mayonnaise
1 T. sugar

Parmesan, Romano cheese
¾ lbs. fried bacon crumbled
3 or 4 hard boiled eggs,
   sliced
3 tomato slices

Break up lettuce and place in large shallow serving dish. Sprinkle next 3 layers of ingredients on top. Spread mayonnaise over top. Sprinkle with sugar. Refrigerate overnight. Before serving add bacon, egg and tomato slices in layers DO NOT TOSS THIS SALAD. Servings should go from bottom to top of bowl. Serves 6.

Kelly Nanna   Baylor University

Grits and Sausage

1 c. grits
3 c. water
1 t. salt
2 T. Pace Picante Sauce

1 lb. Owens Country
Sausage or comparable
pan sausage
1 T. Worcestershire sauce

Boil water with salt. Add grits, lower heat and boil for 5 minutes. Add Worcestershire sauce to the pan and fry the sausage, crumbling into very small pieces. Remove sausage from pan, draining the grease. Mix sausage with the grits and add picante sauce to your taste.

Randall Harris   University of Texas

66

Tuna Spread

1 can of tuna (water packed) 3 t. Mrs. Dash
3 T. mayonnaise   Several slices of cheddar
3 t. paprika   cheese

Combine ingredients. Spread on toast or crackers. Melt cheese slices on top.

Jennifer Platt   **Pepperdine University**

French Toast

2 eggs   1 T. butter
¾ c. cold milk   4 T. sugar
½ t. salt   6 to 8 slices white bread
⅛ t. nutmeg   (slightly stale is even better)

1. With a fork lightly beat eggs, salt, nutmeg, sugar and milk until well mixed.
2. Melt butter (margarine) in frying pan and heat until butter begins to brown.
3. Dip each slice of bread in egg batter until well soaked, and place in frying pan to cook.
4. Cook one side til lightly browned and flip over to brown other side.

Keep French Toast hot in a warm oven until you've cooked all your bread. Serve hot with butter and syrup. Serves 2 or 3.

George H. Zinn III   **Bowdoin College**

Easy Egg Salad Casserole

6 chopped hard boiled eggs   ¼ t. pepper
1 c. mayonnaise   1 c. bread crumbs
¼ c. milk   ½ c. crushed crackers
¼ t. garlic powder   2 T. melted butter

Preheat oven to 400°, and grease large casserole. In a bowl, combine chopped eggs, mayonnaise, milk, garlic powder, pepper and bread crumbs. Spread in casserole. Combine crackers and margarine and sprinkle over casserole. Bake for 20 minutes or until top is golden brown. Makes 4 servings.

Bob Zech   **Georgetown University**

Grilled Cheese, Bacon & Tomato Sandwiches

8 slices bacon
1 ripe tomato, sliced
4 slices cheese, any kind

8 pieces of sandwich bread
Margarine

Fry the bacon first, then drain and allow to crispen. Spread a small amount of margarine on each piece of bread. Take 4 pieces of bread and place equal amounts of cheese, bacon and tomato on each non-buttered side. Place remaining pieces of bread on top and place the sandwiches on a cookie tray. Place in oven on broil until bread is toasted. Turn the sandwiches over and repeat. Makes 4.

Nancy MacWilliams   **Georgetown University**

SUBJECT:

DESSERTS

Peanut Butter Yum-Yums

1 Roll refrigerate "slice and bake" peanut butter cookies
1 pkg. 36 miniature Reese's peanut butter cups.

Follow directions on cookie wrapper—dividing roll into 9 slices and cutting each slice into quarters (36 pieces). Put one quarter into each cup of miniature muffin tin. Bake 10-12 minutes at 375° or until lightly brown. Immediately upon removing from oven, put one Reese's piece into middle of each cookie. Let cool completely before removing from muffin tin.

Katie Fleece   **Louisiana State University**

Congo Bars

1 lb. brown sugar	2¼ c. flour
1 stick + 2 t. margarine or	2 t. baking powder
butter	1 pkg chocolate chips
3 eggs	Nuts if desired
1 t. vanilla	

Melt butter over med-low heat. Stir in brown sugar and vanilla. Add eggs (one at a time). When well-blended add dry ingredients. Stir until smooth. Add chips and nuts. Cook at 350° for 20 minutes (less if you like them gooey). Use 13"x9" pan (greased with butter).

Kim Spaulding   **Dartmouth College**

Banana Pudding

1 small box instant banana	1 t. vanilla extract
pudding	3 bananas, sliced
2 c. milk	

Mix pudding and milk and extract for 2 minutes on high speed. Add bananas, chill.

Mark Dunham   **University of Florida**

Chocolate Crinkles

2 c. granulated sugar
½ c. vegetable oil
4 oz. unsweetened chocolate
  (cooled)
4 t. vanilla

4 eggs
2 c. flour
2 t. baking powder
½ t. salt
½ c. powdered sugar

Mix granulated sugar, oil, chocolate and vanilla. Mix in eggs (one at a time). Stir in flour, baking powder and salt. Cover and refrigerate at least 3 hours. Shape dough into balls by teaspoon. Roll (generously) in powdered sugar. Bake on greased cookie sheets for 10-12 minutes in 350° oven.

Ann Crocker   **Brown University**

Cupcake Brownies

Preheat oven to 325°.
Melt on low heat:

4 sq. semi-sweet chocolate
  and 2 sticks butter
Mix:
1 c. flour
1¾ c. sugar
4 eggs (one at a time, stirring
  as little as possible)

Add:
2 t. vanilla extract
1 c. chopped pecans

Pour into paper cups in muffin tins. Bake at 325° for 25-30 minutes. Note: They don't look done when taken out of oven. Let cool.

Troy Owen   **Stephen F. Austin
                                            State University**

Easy Lemon Wafers

1 box lemon cake mix
1 c. Wesson oil

2 eggs

Mix all ingredients and drop teaspoon size portions on greased cookie sheet. (Cookie sheet only has to be greased once!) Bake at 350° for 8-10 minutes. Delicious and makes a bunch!

Tom Byron   **Georgetown University**

Chocolate Chip Cookies

1 c. Crisco
¾ c. sugar
¾ c. dark brown sugar, packed
2 eggs
2¼ c. flour

Pinch salt
2 t. vanilla
1 t. soda in 1 t. hot water
12 oz. pkg. chocolate chips
1 pkg. Heath Bar Brickle

Cream Crisco and sugars. Add eggs and vanilla. Mix flour and salt. Add to mixture. Add soda. Add chips and brickle. Mix well. Drop by rounded teaspoon onto cookie sheet. Bake at 350° for 10 minutes. Cool slightly. Remove from pan and finish cooling.

Nancy Baker **Ole Miss**

Chocolate Chews

½ c. butter
1⅔ c. sugar
2 t. vanilla
2 eggs
2 squares chocolate

2 c. flour
2 t. baking powder
Salt
⅓ c. milk

Cream butter and sugar. Add vanilla. Beat in eggs. Melt chocolate and add. Combine flour, baking powder and salt. Add dry ingredients, alternating with milk, to creamed mixture. Stir as you add. Chill 2 to 3 hours. Roll dough in small balls. Roll balls in powdered sugar. Bake at 350° for 8 minutes.

Melanie Meador **Baylor University**

Chocolate and Oatmeal Cookies

1 c. sugar
1 c. brown sugar
1 c. shortening
2 eggs
½ t. baking powder

1 t. vanilla
1 t. baking soda
¼ t. salt
2 c. oats
1 pkg. chocolate chips

Cream together the first three ingredients. Beat eggs and add to mixture. Add flour, baking powder, vanilla, baking soda, salt and mix well. Next add oats and chocolate chips. Drop on cookie sheet and bake at 350° for 15 minutes.

Hope Bradberry   **University of Tulsa**

Brownies

1 bar of Baker's Chocolate
75 grams or 2½ oz. butter
1 c. sugar

2 eggs
¾ c. flour

Preheat oven to 375°. Melt the butter and the chocolate together. Remove from stove and put in mixing bowl. Add sugar, eggs and flour. Mix together. Bake in oven for 35-40 minutes. Cut while warm.

Elizabeth Nieroth   **Georgetown University**

Lemon Bars

1 stick butter
1 c. flour

¼ c. powdered sugar

Mix the above and put in 9″ square pan. Bake 15 minutes at 350°.

Mix:
2 eggs, slightly beaten
2 T. lemon juice
2 T. lemon rind, grated

1 c. sugar
2 T. flour
½ t. baking powder

Pour mixture over crust. Bake 25 minutes at 350°. Sprinkle with powdered sugar when hot.

Craig Davis   **Stanford University**

74

Peanut Butter Balls

2 c. crunchy peanut butter
½ lb. margarine
1½ c. confectioners sugar
4 c. Rice Krispies

12 oz. Hershey Bars (1½ bars)
12 oz. semi-sweet chocolate
   chips
¼ stick parafin

Mix together peanut butter, sugar and margarine. Fold in Rice Krispies with a wooden spoon. Refrigerate the mixture for one hour. Melt together the chocolates and parafin. Make peanut butter mixture into small balls. Dip and roll the balls in the chocolate mixture. Place on wax paper and refrigerate. Makes two dozen.

Julie Reeside   **Wayne State University**

Peanut Krispie Cookie Things

1 c. sugar   1 c. white Karo syrup

Bring to boil and add:
12 oz. chunky peanut butter

Pour this over
5 c. Rice Krispies

Shape into balls. Keep in air-tight container.

Susan Gaetz   **Vanderbilt University**

Oatmeal Crisp

1½ c. brown sugar
1½ c. butter (3 sticks) at room
   temperature

3 c. oatmeal, uncooked
1½ c. flour
1½ t. baking soda

Preheat oven to 350°. Place all the ingredients in a large bowl. Mix with your hands. Knead until there aren't any lumps of butter. Roll dough into small balls, three inches apart. Flatten gently with a small fork. Bake 10-12 minutes at 350°. Cool before removing from cookie sheet. Makes 6 dozen cookies.

Patrick Linbeck   **University of Notre Dame**

Hello Dolly Cookies

6 T. margarine
1 c. crushed vanilla wafers
1 pkg. (6 oz.) semi-sweet
   chocolate chips

1 can (4 oz.) Angel Flake
   coconut
1 c. chopped pecans
1 can (15 oz.) Eagle Brand
   Sweetened Condensed Milk

Melt margarine in a 9x13 Pyrex glass pan. Add vanilla wafer crumbs and press them into a very thin layer. Over crumbs, sprinkle chocolate chips, the coconut and then pecans. Evenly pour (lightly) condensed milk over all. Bake at 325° for about 30 minutes. Let sit for a couple hours before devouring. It's worth the wait.

Eleanor H. Hitchcock　　　　　　**Ohio Wesleyan University**

Lemon Bars

Heat the oven to 350°.

Mix together:
2 c. flour

½ c. confectioners sugar
¾ c. melted butter

Press the above into a 9x13 pan. Bake for 15 minutes.

While the crust is baking, mix together:

2 c. sugar
4 T. flour
3 eggs

1 t. baking powder
6-10 T. lemon juice (use 10 T.
   if you like lemon!)

Pour over crust and bake 25 minutes more. Dust with confectioners sugar. Makes 24 bars.

Stephanie Moore　　　　　　**Oakland University**

Mint Brownies

1 box brownie mix	1 can ready-to-spread
1 can ready-to-spread vanilla	chocolate icing
icing	1 small bottle peppermint
	extract

Make brownies, following directions on box (use a 9x13 pan). Allow to cool completely. Mix peppermint extract into vanilla icing. Ice the brownies with mint icing. Use the whole can to create a ¼" thick layer of white icing. Chill white-iced brownies in freezer until icing is set. Remove and ice with chocolate icing to create a ¼" layer of icing. Keep dessert chilled and covered until ½ hour before serving. Great with ice cream.

Patrick Linbeck   **University of Notre Dame**

Chocolate Chip Cookies

Blend:	Beat and add 2 eggs, one at a time.
1 c. shortening	2¼ c. flour
¾ c. sugar	1 t. baking soda
¾ c. brown sugar	1 t. salt
Mix well	
1 t. vanilla	
½ t. water	

Mix all ingredients very well and stir in 1 large package of chocolate Nestle's Chips. Bake at 375° for 9-11 minutes.

Shayna Goldstein   **Southern Methodist University**

Peach Cobbler — Easy

1 c. sugar	1 stick margarine
1 c. milk	1 egg
¾ c. flour	1 large can sliced peaches
2 t. baking powder	Dash of cinnamon

Melt margarine in pan. Mix dry ingredients with egg and milk in another bowl. Add this to margarine in pan and mix. Pour into greased dish (10x6). Pour peaches (juice and all) over mixture. Bake 1 hour at 350°.

Susan Gaetz   **Vanderbilt University**

Pecan Pie

1 c. corn syrup
½ c. light brown sugar
3 eggs

1 t. vanilla
¼ t. salt
1 c. shelled pecans
1 frozen pie shell

Mix all ingredients well and pour into unbaked shell. Cook at 350° for 50 minutes.

Patrick Linbeck   **University of Notre Dame**

Derby Pie

1 frozen pie shell
½ c. melted butter
¼ c. cornstarch
2 eggs
1 c. sugar

4 T. bourbon
1 c. chopped pecans
6 oz. pkg. chocolate chips
1 T. vanilla

Combine butter, corn starch, beaten eggs, sugar and bourbon in a saucepan. Heat until butter is melted. Cool. Add chocolate chips and vanilla. Pour into pie shell and bake at 350° for 50 minutes.

Tony Gray   **Texas Christian University**

Raspberry-Peach Ice

1 part peaches - frozen   2 parts raspberries - frozen

Put frozen peaches and raspberries in blender and blend with just enough water to let it mix smoothly. (About 2 T. or so.) Serve alone or with whipped cream. (This is wonderful and very low in calories!)

Martha Harrington   **Stanford University**

Blueberry Pie

1 can blueberry pie filling	1 box Jiffy yellow cake mix or
1 stick butter	½ box Duncan Hines yellow
1 small pkg. pecans	cake mix

This recipe is for a microwave. Melt butter in glass pie pan. When melted, pour off all but one tablespoon. SAVE THIS! Spread pie filling bottom of pan, sprinkle with cake mix, drizzle butter over all and sprinkle with pecans. Microwave on high for 10 minutes. Serve warm with ice cream.

Lisa Platt   University of Arizona

Apple Pie

Mix and roll out, makes 4 pie crusts.

Pie crust:	1 t. salt
3 c. flour	½ c. water
1 c. + 2 t. shortening	
1 t. baking powder	

6 c. apples	¼ t nutmeg
¾ c. sugar	½ t salt
¼ c. brown sugar	⅓ c. cream
2 T. flour	3 T. butter
½ t. cinnamon	9″ pie shell with top

Peel and cut apples. Mix dry ingredients together. In pie shell alternate apples with dry ingredients 3 times. Butter and pour cream in center. Bake 400° for 1 hour.

Holly Chamness   Southern Methodist University

Key Lime Pie

1 can sweetened condensed milk (Eagle Brand)	Cool Whip (9 oz. - 6 oz. best)
1 small can limeade frozen concentrate	1 graham cracker crust
	Green food coloring, a drop

Put 20-22 graham crackers in a blender with ½ stick of butter. Blend until fine crumbs. Press into a pie shell to make a crust.

Mix limeade with Eagle Brand and fold in Cool Whip. Add green food coloring, pour into pie shell. Chill. Serves 5-6.

Ann Sherwood   Stanford Univeristy

Granny's Blueberry Pie

1 8 oz. cream cheese
1 9 oz. Cool Whip
1 c. powdered sugar

1 can blueberry pie filling
1 graham cracker pie crust
9"

Blend 20 graham crackers with 2 T. butter in blender to make a pie crust. Press firmly to cover pie pan bottom and sides. Cream powdered sugar and cream cheese. Fold in Cool Whip. Pour into pie shell. Let chill for several hours, then pour blueberry pie filling (which has been chilled) over this. You may substitute cherry pie filling for the blueberry.

Teri Dale   **College of William & Mary**

Grasshopper Pie

24 finely crushed Oreos
¼ c. margarine, melted
¼ c. creme de menthe

1 jar Kraft Marshmallow
  creme
2 c. heavy cream, whipped

1. Roll out crumbs between 2 pieces of waxed paper, using 6-8 oreos at a time.
2. Melt margarine in pan over low heat. Combine cookie crumbs in a bowl.
3. Press cookie mixture into bottom of a 9" spring pan (or something comparable) saving some crumbs for topping.
4. Carefully and gradually add creme de menthe in a mixing bowl to marshmallow creme. (Use a hot spatula to remove creme.)
5. Chill mixer beaters and clean bowl in freezer for 5 minutes or so. Then whip the cream. (Do not lift beaters out of bowl while whipping the cream.)
6. Gently fold whipped cream into marshmallow creme and creme de menthe.
7. Pour whole "mess" into pan and sprinkle with oreo crumbs.
8. Wrap in foil and freeze overnight.

Jennifer Jones   **College of William & Mary**

Hershey Bar Pie

6 almond Hershey bars
18 large marshmallows
½ c. milk

½ pint whipping cream
20-25 graham crackers
3 T butter

Mix graham crackers and butter in a blender until fine crumbs. Press into pie to form a shell.

Melt first three ingredients, stirring constantly. Let cool. Whip whipping cream. Fold in chocolate mixture. Pour into graham cracker pie crust. Refrigerate several hours. It's very rich so can serve eight.

Denise DeCell   Texas Tech University

Freshman 15 Fudge

1 box powdered sugar
1 can Pet Evaporated Milk
⅓ c. butter
¼ t salt
¼ t. baking powder

1½ c. miniature
   marshmallows
½ t. vanilla
Pecans (if desired)

Mix all contents except for marshmallows, vanilla and nuts. Bring to a boil over medium heat. Let boil for 5 minutes, stirring all the time the fudge is over heat. After boiling for 5 minutes, take off the heat and add 1½ c. miniature marshmallows, vanilla and nuts (if desired). Let set on the counter. If fudge takes too long to set, you can put it in the fridge for a little while.

Missy Kroll   Baylor University

U.V.A. Fudge

1 12 oz. P-Nut Butter Chips
1 12 oz. Heath Bar Brickle
   Chips

1 11½ oz. milk chocolate
   chips
1 can condensed milk

Melt chocolate chips and p-nut butter chips in condensed milk with 1 T. margarine. Fold in brickle chips and spread on greased wax paper laid out on jelly roll pan. Cool. Cut into squares.

Lisa Crosswell   University of Virginia

Chocolate No-Bakes

1 c. sugar
½ c. cocoa
⅓ c. milk
½ c. butter

3 c. oats
½ c. peanut butter
1 t. vanilla

Mix sugar, cocoa, milk and butter in saucepan and heat till boiling, stirring constantly. Boil for 1 minute. Remove from heat and add oats, peanut butter and vanilla. Drop by teaspoonful onto clean surface. Cool till set.

Laura Winkelmaier   **Trinity University**

Ice Cream Puffs

Puffs:
1 c. water
½ c. butter
1 c. sifted flour
4 eggs

Filling:
Your favorite ice cream

Topping:
Chocolate or butterscotch
  sauce or warm strawberry
  jam

Heat water and butter to a rolling boil. Stir flour in all at once. Stir vigorously over low heat until mixture leaves the pan and forms into a ball (about 1 minute). Remove from heat. Add eggs, one at a time, beating thoroughly after each addition. Beat mixture until smooth and velvety. Drop from spoon onto ungreased baking sheet. Bake at 400° for 45-50 minutes until puffs are dry. Remove from oven and allow to cool slowly. When cool, cut off tops with a sharp knife. Scoop out any filaments of soft dough. Fill with ice cream. Replace tops and pour desired topping over puffs. (Add chopped nuts or berries if you wish.)

Mimi Kilinger   **University of Virginia**

Fudge

3 c. sugar
6 T. cocoa

Mix together:
2 T. Karo syrup
1½ c. milk

Stir and put on medium heat. Cook until it forms soft balls. Add ½ stick butter and vanilla flavoring, 3 T. peanut butter. Beat until shiny and pour into a pan. Cool and cut.

Amy Hallgarth   **Baylor University**

Microwave Fudge

1 lb. box powdered sugar
¼ c. milk
1 t. vanilla
¼ c. cocoa
1 stick of butter
Nuts (optional)

Pour sugar into 8x8 square glass pan. Add cocoa, milk and butter. Slice butter into 4 or 5 pieces and dot around on mixture. Do not stir. Put into microwave for 3 to 4 minutes. Stir vigorously. Add vanilla and nuts. Refrigerate for 1 hour only. Remove, cut and enjoy!

Leslie Hollingsworth   **Trinity University**

Microwave Chocolate Nut Candy

12 oz. Nestle's butterscotch
morsels
6 oz. Nestle's chocolate
morsels
12 oz. salted peanuts or
pecans
Optional small bag of small
marshmallows

Microwave 2 types of morsels on high 2-3 minutes. Mix to blend. Add peanuts (and marshmallows). Stir. Drop by teaspoon onto waxed paper. Let cool. Serve.

Katherine West   **University of Mississippi**

Lemon Cream

2 cartons heavy cream,
also called cream for
whipping
2 T. grated fresh lemon rind
3 T. fresh lemon juice
1 c. sugar

Dissolve sugar in cream, by stirring 4 minutes. Add the other ingredients and blend. Divide mixture into wine glasses and place in freezer. Take out 15 minutes before serving. Serve with Pepperidge Farm Cookies.

Lisa Platt   **University of Arizona**

Chow Mein Noodle Candy

1 can chow mein noodles
1 pkg. butterscotch chips
small
2 pkg. chocolate chips,
small

Melt above ingredients. Mix in chow mein noodles and stir. Drop when stiff on wax paper and let cool.

Sherrill Baxter   **University of Texas at Austin**

Easy Caramels

1 c. butter
2¼ c. light brown sugar
1 dash salt
1 c. light corn syrup

1 c. Eagle Brand Milk
1 t. vanilla
1 c. chopped nuts

Melt butter in heavy 3 quart saucepan. Add brown sugar and salt, mixing thoroughly. Add syrup, then gradually add Eagle Brand milk, stirring constantly. Cook and stir over medium heat until candy reaches 245° on a candy thermometer (about 15-20 minutes). Pour in buttered 9x9 pan. Cool. Cut into squares and wrap individually in wax paper.

Lisa Noble   Stephen F. Austin State University

Chocolate Icebox Pudding

½ c. butter
1½ c. powdered sugar
4 egg yolks
4 egg whites, beaten stiff
8 oz. pkg. German Sweet
    chocolate, melted

½ t. vanilla
Juice of ½ lemon
1 cup pecans, chopped
Vanilla wafer crumbs

Mix butter and powdered sugar until very light. Add egg yolks, chocolate, vanilla, lemon juice. Beat egg whites until stiff but not dry. Fold in chocolate mixture and nuts. Now line pan with vanilla wafer crumbs. Pour ½ chocolate mixture over this, more vanilla wafer crumbs over top then more chocolate. Refrigerate overnight and serve with whipped cream.

Ann Carmady   Ole Miss

Coffee & Chocolate Chip Sundae

Coffee ice cream
Semi-sweet chocolate chips

Hot fudge sauce
Whipped cream topping

In a bowl, place several scoops of ice cream. Cover with heated fudge sauce and chocolate chips. Add topping (and nuts, if desired).

Heather O'Neill   Georgetown University

Chocolate Chip Cake

1 yellow cake mix
1 t. vanilla
12 oz. pkg. chocolate chips
4 eggs
2 sm. pkgs. instant chocolate pudding
½ c. oil
½ c. water

Mix all ingredients together for 2 minutes with mixer. Add chocolate chips. Pour in greased and floured Bundt pan. Bake at 325° for 75 minutes. Cool. Dust with powdered sugar.

Amanda Justice   **Randolph-Macon Woman's College**

Chocolate Pound Cake

1 Duncan Hines Deluxe II yellow cake mix
2 small pkgs. instant chocolate pudding
½ c. oil
1½ c. water
4 eggs, beaten
1 t. vanilla
1 6 oz. pkg. chocolate chips

Beat ingredients (except chocolate chips) for 2 minutes. Fold in chocolate chips. Bake in 350° oven for 1 hour. Let cool 15 minutes. Use a large loaf pan.

Sherrill Baxter   **University of Texas at Austin**

Cocoa Cake

2 c. sugar
2 c. flour
1 stick butter
½ c. Crisco
4 T. cocoa
1 c. water
2 eggs
½ c. buttermilk
1 t. soda
1 t. cinnamon
1 t. vanilla

In large bowl combine sugar and flour. In saucepan melt butter, Crisco, cocoa, water and bring to boil (just to melt). Add to flour and sugar mixture along with eggs, buttermilk, soda, cinnamon and vanilla. Mix well and pour into oblong greased and floured pan. Bake at 400° for 20 minutes.

Allison Harter   **Southern Methodist University**

A-C's Cheese Cake

1 box graham cracker crust
  mix
1 pkg. (8 oz.) cream cheese
1 pkg. (3 oz.) cream cheese
¾ c. sugar
2 eggs
2 t. vanilla

Topping:
1 c. sour cream
6 T. sugar
1 t. vanilla

Preheat oven to 325°. Prepare graham cracker crust using directions on box. (I omit the sugar.) Mix other ingredients. Put crust in 9" or 10" pan. Pour in cheese mixture. Bake in oven for 30 minutes or until *almost* firm. *Cool* for 5 minutes. Pour on topping that has been mixed thoroughly. Bake 10 minutes more. Chill for 4 or 5 hours. Instead of the sour cream topping, canned fruit pie filling can be sed. I enjoy this recipe because it is very fast, but guests think it takes hours to prepare. It freezes well.

Ann-Claire Anderson　　　　　　　　**Trinity University**

Chocolate Sheet Cake

2 c. flour
2 c. sugar
2 sticks margarine
4 T. cocoa
2 c. water

1 t. vanilla
1 t. soda
½ c. buttermilk
2 eggs

Preheat oven to 350°. In bowl mix flour and sugar and set aside. On the stove, melt margarine and add cocoa and water. Mix this with flour and sugar. On the side, mix the buttermilk with the baking soda and let rise (double in size). Add vanilla, eggs, and buttermilk. Pour into 8 x 11 greased and floured cake pan. Bake for 25 minutes at 350°.

Icing:
1 stick margarine
4 T. cocoa

5 T. milk
¾ box powdered sugar
1 c. chopped pecans (optional)

Boil in a saucepan the margarine, cocoa and milk until creamy. Add powdered sugar and pecans. When cake has cooled, cover it with icing.

Kyle Davis　　　　　　　　**South Texas State University**

Angel Delight

2 6 oz. pkgs. chocolate chips   4 eggs
    or   ½ c. sugar
1 12 oz. pkg. chocolate chips   1 t. vanilla
1 pt. whipping cream   1 Angel Food cake
                             Chopped pecans

Melt in double boiler. Beat 4 egg yolks and pour some of hot chocolate over them and then all melted chocolate chips. Stir and *let cool.* Beat 4 egg whites until stiff and add slowly ½ c. sugar, and 1 t. vanilla. Fold cooled chocolate mixture into egg whites, then fold in 1 pt. whipped cream.

Break angel food cake into pieces, place in bottom of 9x13 Pyrex dish. Pour chocolate mixture over angel cake and sprinkle with chopped pecans. Refrigerate, overnight is better.

Laura Smith   **University of Mississippi**

Mississippi Mud Cake

4 eggs   1 t. vanilla
2 c. sugar   1 c. coconut
2 sticks melted butter   1-2 c. pecans
1½ c. sifted flour   1 jar marshmallow creme
⅓ c. cocoa

Beat eggs and sugar until thick. Mix other ingredients (except marshmallow creme) and add to egg and sugar mixture. Mix well. Bake in a 13x9 pan that has been greased and floured for 30 minutes. Remove from oven and spread at once with a jar of marshmallow creme.

Icing: 1 box powdered sugar
1 stick melted margarine   1 c. nuts (pecans)
6 T. milk   1 t. vanilla
⅓ c. cocoa

Add all ingredients to melted margarine. Beat well. Spread gently over marshmallow creme while warm. Serves 10.

Lisa Jones   **Smith College**

Rum Cake

1 c. chopped pecans
1 pkg. yellow cake mix
  (w/pudding in it)
4 eggs
¼ c. water
¼ c. oil
½ c. Bacardi lite rum

Glaze:
1 c. sugar
¼ c. water
½ c. butter

Stir ingredients (except pecans) until boiling and let boil for 5 minutes, stirring constantly. Stir in rum. Place pecans in bottom of greased bundt pan. Mix other ingredients and place on top of pecans. Cook 1 hour at 325° then cool for 15 minutes. Pour glaze over cake.

Marie Fondren   **Southern Methodist University**

Bacardi Rum Cake

Cake:
1 c. chopped nuts
1 yellow 18½ oz. cake mix
1 3¾ pkg. Jello Instant
  Pudding (vanilla)
4 eggs
½ c. water
½ c. Wesson oil
½ c. dark rum

Glaze:
¼ lb. butter
¼ c. water
1 c. sugar
½ c. rum

Sprinkle nuts in bottom of pan; pour batter over. Bake at 325°. Glaze - melt butter in saucepan. Stir in water and sugar. Boil for 5 minutes. Stir constantly. Remove from heat and add rum. Pour over cake.

DeAnn Shelton   **Oklahoma State Universty**

Magic Mousse

1 6 oz. pkg. Nestle's bits
¼ c. boiling water
1 egg

½ c. heavy cream
1 t. vanilla

In a blender combine chocolate bits and boiling water and whirl at high speed 15 seconds (until smooth). Add egg, cream and vanilla and whirl at high speed for 30 seconds. Stop blender, scrape sides and whirl for 15 more seconds. Spoon into individual cups and chill for several hours. Serve and enjoy.

Cory Schia   **University of Houston**

Texas Gold Bars

1 box yellow cake mix
  (without pudding)
1 egg slightly beaten
1 stick margarine, melted

Topping:
1 8 oz. pkg. cream cheese
1 box powdered sugar
2 eggs, slightly beaten

Mix cake mix, eggs & margarine. Then mix topping ingredients together. Pour over top of cake mixture. Bake at 300° for 50 minutes. Let cool before serving.

Sheryl Durkee   **Ole Miss**

Wine Cake

1 Duncan Hines Yellow
  Cake Mix
4 eggs
1 small pkg. vanilla
  instant pudding

¾ c. Wesson oil
¾ c. port or sherry
1 t. nutmeg

Beat eggs till light, then add dry and liquid ingredients alternately. Beat at medium speed for 5 minutes. Pour into greased bundt pan and bake at 350° for 45 minutes. Cool 10 minutes, remove from pan, and sprinkle with powdered sugar.

Kathie Lewis   **University of Tulsa**

Ooey Gooey Butter Cake

1 yellow or white cake mix
½ stick butter
3 eggs

8 oz. pkg. Philadelphia
  cream cheese
1 box confectioners sugar
1 t. vanilla

Mix until crumbly, cake mix, butter and 1 egg. Place in oblong pan as crust. Set aside. In a bowl combine cream cheese, confectioners sugar, 2 eggs and beat until blended. Add vanilla; stir. Pour over crust in oblong pan. Bake for 20-30 minutes on 350°.

Suzanne O'Neal   Baylor University

Sour Cream Coffee Cake
(Freezes Well)

Batter:
1 box Duncan Hines white
  cake mix
¾ c. Wesson oil

4 eggs
½ c. sugar
1 c. sour cream
1 t. vanilla

Grease and flour a tube pan. Mix all above ingredients together and beat for 3 minutes at medium speed. Pour half of batter into tube pan. Sprinkle half of topping mix on batter. Add remaining batter. Add remaining topping. Bake at 350° for 50 minutes or less. Start testing at 40 minutes. (Don't over cook.) Remove from oven and pour glaze over cake while hot. Cool for 1 hour before cutting.

Topping: Mix well
½ c. nuts, chopped
3 T. brown sugar
2 t. cinnamon

Glaze:
1 c. powdered sugar
Milk to moisten

Start with 1 t. milk and gradually add more as needed to glaze. Glaze should be thick but thin enough to dribble on cake.

Ronnie Jacobe   Princeton University

90

SUBJECT:

BREAD & ROLLS

Tea Rolls

1 c. butter
1 c. sour cream

2 c. self-rising flour

Cream butter by cutting into flour. Add sour cream. Drop by teaspoons into muffin tins (preferably the miniature kind). Bake at 425° for 10 minutes. Makes one dozen.

Jill Shaffner   **University of Texas at Austin**

Beer Muffins

3½ c. Bisquick
1 can beer

¼ c. sugar

Combine above in mixing bowl. Let stand 30 minutes. Pour into buttered muffin tins. Bake at 400° 10 to 15 minutes. Makes 2 dozen.

Lisa Platt   **University of Arizona**

Bran Bread

3 c. flour
¼ c. sugar
1 t. salt

1 t. baking soda
1 t. baking powder
1 c. bran buds

Mix above ingredients. Add 1½ (plus a little) cups of buttermilk and 2 T. molasses. Bake in 350° oven for 55 minutes. Remove and cover with butter. Makes one loaf.

Ann McConigle   **Brown University**

Banana Nut Bread

2 c. flour
1½ c. sugar
½ c. shortening
2 eggs
1 t. vanilla

1 t. baking soda
4 T. buttermilk
3 crushed bananas (mash with fork)
½ c. pecans

Mix sugar, shortening and bananas together. Add eggs, soda and buttermilk. Add flour, nuts and vanilla. Bake in a loaf pan, well greased and floured. Bake 45 minutes at 350°.

Peter Stinner   **Trinity University**

Struesel Muffins

Cake:
1½ c. sifted flour
3 t. baking powder
¼ t. salt
¾ c. sugar
¼ c. margarine
1 egg
½ c. milk

Filling: Mix together
2 t. flour
2 t. cinnamon
½ c. brown sugar
2 T. melted margarine
½ c. chopped nuts

Mix cake dry ingredients, cut in margarine with pastry blender. Blend in beaten egg and milk. Pour into greased and floured muffin tins. Fill about ½ way. Top with filling. Take knife and swirl, punch in filling. Bake at 375° for 15-20 minutes. They freeze well. Makes 2 dozen.

Lisa Noble   **Stephen F. Austin State University**

Irish Bread

3 c. flour
½ c. sugar
1 t. salt
3 t. baking powder

3 T. butter
1 c. milk
1 egg
1 c. raisins

Mix flour, sugar, salt, baking powder and raisins. Mix in butter with hands. Add milk and eggs; mix well. Bake at 350° in buttered and floured pan for approximately 50 minutes. Makes one loaf.

Ann McGonigle   **Brown University**

Beer Bread

3 c. self-rising flour
½ c. sugar

1 can beer at room temp.
  (12 oz. light)
¼ lb. butter, melted

Preheat oven to 350°. Mix flour and sugar. Add beer and mix well. Spoon into greased 9x5 loaf pan. Bake at 350° for 45 minutes. Remove from oven and pour melted butter over loaf. Return to oven for 15 minutes. (This is so good and looks harder than it is!) Makes one loaf.

Martha Harrington   **Stanford University**

Sausage Bread

Bread dough to equal 2 loaves (found in frozen food section)

2 lbs. sweet Italian sausage (11 oz., if links, remove casing)

2-3 good sized onions, chopped

¾ lb. Swiss cheese, shredded
¾ lb. mozzarella, shredded
4 eggs, beaten
¼ c. grated Parmesan cheese
Salt and Pepper
Oil
Parsley

Brown sausage and drain; add onions, saute. Stretch large cookie sheet (with sides) with ½ the dough. Pat oil on dough. Mix eggs with sausage; stir in cheeses and spread on dough. Roll out rest of dough; put on top of sausage mixture. Rub oil on top. Sprinkle with parsley, grated cheese, salt and pepper. Bake at 400° for 1-1½ hours.

Mary Bresnicky

**Yale University
Notre Dame Law School**

Nut Bread

1 beaten egg
Pinch salt
½ c. milk
½ c. water
¾ c. sugar-add to beaten egg

Alternate 2 c. flour with liquid
2 t. baking powder
¾ c. nuts
3 t. vanilla

Bake at 325° for ½ hour, after loaf has risen, increase to 350° to brown. (Bake in greased/floured bread pan.) Makes 1 loaf.

Lynn Drury

Texas Christian University

Bran Muffins

1¼ c. all purpose flour
1 T. baking powder
½ t. salt
1 c. all bran cereal

1 c. milk
1 egg
3 T. vegetable oil or
   shortening
½ c. nuts, raisins or sugar

1. Stir together flour, baking powder, salt (sugar). Set aside.
2. Measure all bran cereal, milk into large mixing bowl. Stir to combine. Let stand 1 to 2 minutes or until cereal is softened. Add egg and oil. Beat well.
3. Add flour mixture, stirring only until combined. Portion batter evenly into 12 greased 2½" muffin pan.
4. Bake at 400° for 25 minutes or until lightly browned. Makes one dozen.

Marsha Moore　　　　　　　**Oakland Community College**

SUBJECT:

PARTY MENUS

Some Party Menus
for Special Occasions!

Brunch for a Bunch

Brunch is a wonderful party to serve in your kitchen, particularly at an old table covered with a colorful piece of oil cloth. Set our your cold drinks on the counter tops: pitchers of orange juice, tomato juice and milk with a welcoming pitcher of your favorite Bloody Mary concoction (Mr. and Mrs. "T" with fresh lime and celery stalks makes delicious Virgin Bloody Mary's.) Remember to abide by the appropriate laws governing liquor use by your school and state.

Fill a bowl with the freshest fruit you can find, all left in their natural skins . . . oranges, apples, strawberries, grapes, bananas, pears, peaches . . . whatever is ripe and in season. Allow one piece of fruit per person. Melons, such as honeydew and cantalope can be cut into small wedges for finger food.

The stove top can be part of your serving table to keep things warm. Keep pans of water on top of stove at a low simmer. Place those things that you need to keep warm in tins and place on top of the simmering water.

On the table place a pot of hot coffee and interesting tea such as a smokey Lapsang Souchong with your other delicious menu choices. This is a good comfortable time to enjoy those special friendships. Don't be surprised if your guests are still lingering at sunset!

Menu

Fresh Fruit
Bagels, cream cheese and smoked salmon
French toast a l'orange
Sausage
Coffee, tea, juices and Bloody Mary's

Bagels, Cream Cheese and Smoked Salmon
Slice bagels (in the winter, warm them in a 200° oven for 15 minutes. Wrap in foil and place in a tin over simmering water.)

99

Spread bagels with cream cheese. (Whipped cream cheese is easier to spread and may be found in the dairy department at the grocery.)

Top bagels with thin slices of smoked salmon - ¼ pound will serve 8. If salmon is not in your budget, use thin slices of tomato and thin slices of red onion instead. Sprinkle with basil.

Sausage
Brown and serve sausages are ready in minutes. Simply follow the directions on the package. Allow 2-3 sausages per person.

French Toast a l'orange
8 slices of thick, slightly stale white bread	½ c. milk
	½ stick butter or margarine
4 eggs	Good English marmalade

In an electric skillet (if using the stove, watch carefully so that butter or margarine doesn't burn), melt butter or margarine, until bubbly. Beat together eggs and milk. Dip each piece of bread into the egg/milk mixture and put into the skillet. Brown on both sides. Spread marmalade generously on top of each slice and keep warm on top of stove until ready to serve. Serves 8.

Party for a Crew

Having a group of 12 friends for dinner may sound overwhelming and expensive. However, the following menu is affordable, festive and provides a setting that is both relaxing and interesting. This is the perfect menu to celebrate spring!

Menu

Brie cheese with crackers and dried apricots
Indian Cheese Ball
Ten Boy Curry with Minute Rice and Condiments
Sundaes

Indian Cheese Ball

3 large pkgs. (8 oz. each)   ½ c. mixed chopped nuts
   cream cheese   1½ t. curry powder
¾ c. chutney   Shredded coconut

Combine first 4 ingredients. Shape into a ball. Roll ball in coconut. Serve with crackers.

Ten Boy Curry

2 onions, sliced   2 t. curry powder
2 apples, diced   ¼ c. flour
¾ stick margarine   2 c. milk
1 c. raisins   4 c. or more of cooked
3 c. chicken broth (in cans)   chicken, diced

Saute onion and apple in margarine. Add raisins and broth. Mix curry powder and flour and add to milk, stirring well. Pour into onion/apple mixture and stir over low heat until creamy. Add chicken. Serve over rice with a selection of accompaniments.

Sundaes

Place a bowl of ice cream balls on the table with dishes of fresh strawberries or peaches and a dish of chocolate sauce.

Condiments for Curry

Always serve your curry with an array of accompaniments such as:

chopped cherry tomatoes
chopped green onions
flaked coconut
chutney
chopped peanuts
raisins
sliced green and/or ripe olives
chopped green peppers
chopped apples tossed in yogurt
sliced avocados tossed in lime juice
pineapple juice
French fried onion rings (from a can)
chopped sweet pickles
chopped cucumbers tossed in yogurt
steamed snow peas, cut in half

Use your imagination. You may have something in the refrigerator left from a picnic that you can add. Place each condiment in a separate bowl with a spoon. Each guest creates his/her own curry.

After-Glow

On a chilly winter's evening following the school's production of Sheridan's "School for Scandal" avoid the mundane pizza and beer routine and try:

Menu

Assorted Sausages
Mustards
Spinach Salad
Raspberry Sherbert with Hot Fudge Sauce

Assorted Sausages
Choose an assortment of fully cooked sausages such as smoked sausage links, frankfurters, kielbasa, knockwursts, and bratwursts. Allow 2 to 3 sausages per person.

2 c. water	4 T. butter

Pierce the skins of the sausages to prevent them from bursting while cooking. Cook them in the water in a heavy skillet for 20 minutes.

Discard the water and add the butter to the skillet with the sausages. Brown the sausages for several minutes.

Serve on a platter with an array of mustards such as Dijon, honey mustard, "Mucky Duck," wine mustard or herb-flavored mustards. Serves 6.

Spinach Salad

1 cello pkg. fresh spinach	1 medium red onion, sliced
1 can (5 oz.) water chestnuts,	into thin rings
drained	8 strips of bacon, cooked
	and crumbled

Remove stems from spinach and discard. Wash the leaves and spin dry or carefully pat dry with paper towels. Break into bite-size pieces. Combine the spinach, water chestnuts, onion rings and bacon. Cover the bowl and refrigerate as long as four hours.

Dressing

½ c. water   1 egg, slightly beaten
½ c. vinegar   1 t. dry mustard
½ c. sugar

Combine the above in a small sauce pan. Heat to a boiling point, but do not boil. Cook for two minutes. Set aside.

Combine the salad and dressing just before serving. Serves 6.

Sweetheart Soirée

For that perfect friend, that special night, that sentimental, romantic . . . whether it be Valentine's Day or dinner after a rainy day tromp through Central Park. You can set the stage . . . for an encore!

Menu

Chicken Veronique
Stuffed Tomatoes
Strawberry Pie
Champagne

Chicken Veronique

1 large chicken breast per person, split and boned
10½ oz. can mushroom soup
¼ c. dry white wine
Ground pepper, to taste
½ c. sour cream
1 small can white grapes, drained

Place chicken breasts in a heat-proof serving dish. Mix soup, wine, pepper and sour cream in a bowl. Spread over breasts. Add grapes. Bake at 350° for 45 minutes. Serves 2.

Stuffed Tomatoes

2 ripe tomatoes
¼ c. sliced mushrooms, canned
1 T. soy sauce
½ c. thawed, chopped spinach drained
2 strips bacon, cooked and crumbled

Cut off top ¼ of tomato and gently scoop out the meat. Mix mushrooms, soy sauce, spinach and bacon with the tomato meat. Stuff into tomato shell. Bake at 400° for 10-12 minutes. Serves 2.

Strawberry Pie

1 prepared pie crust, baked   1 pt. fresh strawberries

Place strawberries in pie crust.

Glaze:
1 c. strawberries
3 T. cornstarch
Water
Juice of 1 lemon

Mix sugar and cornstarch until fine. Add ⅓ c. water and lemon juice to the mixture. Simmer strawberries and ⅔ c. water. Add cornstarch mixture. Boil until thick (2-3 minutes). Pour over berries in the crust.

Frisbees, Kites and Blankets

That first day of spring!

> *"Of how this spring of love resembleth*
> *The uncertain glory of an April day!*
> *Which now shows all the beauty of the sun*
> *And by and bye a cloud takes all away."*

Shakespeare—Two Gentlemen of Verona

Warm sunshine and a good breeze. Pack your kites and frisbees and head to the open spaces. The glory of such an April day is assured!

Menu

Ants on a Log
Egg salad sandwiches
Potato chips
Delphie's treats

Ants on a Log

celery   raisins, plain or golden
peanut butter

Allow one celery stalk per person. Clean stalk. Stuff with peanut butter and place raisins on the peanut butter.

Egg Salad Sandwiches

6 hard boiled eggs, chopped   Pepper to taste
4 green onions, chopped fine   ½ c. alfalfa sprouts
4 T. green pepper, chopped   1 c. sunflower seeds
  fine   12 slices of whole wheat
⅓ c. mayonnaise or more   bread
  to taste

Mix hard boiled eggs with onion, green pepper, and mayonnaise and sprouts. Spread mixture on thick slices of whole wheat bread which has been spread with a thin layer of mayonnaise. Roll edges in sunflower seeds. Serves 6.

Delphie's Treats

2 6 oz. pkgs. of butterscotch   1 can Chinese noodles
  morsels   1 can chopped nuts
1 6 oz. pkg of chocolate
  morsels

Melt morsels over low heat. Add noodles and nuts. Drop by spoonfuls on waxed paper and allow to cool. Makes 2 dozen.

Vegetarian Caper

A perfect menu after the holidays or for those who wish to avoid meat and poultry.

Menu

Cucumber slices topped with herb cheese
Vegetable salad
French bread
    or
Large Idaho potatoes with condiments
Steamed fresh asparagus
Tray of fresh fruits, cheese and crackers

Vegetable Salad

1 c. cherry tomatoes, cut
  in half
½ lb. fresh mushrooms, sliced
  vertically
1 zucchini, sliced in rounds
1 can tiny carrots, drained
1 can black pitted olives

1-2 c. fresh cauliflower,
  broken into flowerettes
1 green pepper, cut into strips
6 green onions, cut into pieces
¼ lb. feta cheese
1 bottle Wishbone Italian
  dressing

Combine all ingredients except cheese. Marinate for 24 hours in the Italian dressing. Toss with cheese just before serving. Serves 8.

Idaho Potato

1 potato per person

Condiments:
Bowls of sour cream, chopped onions, grated cheese, chopped chives or green onions, butter, chopped cucumbers, "lumpfish" caviar (much more affordable than Beluga!)

Wash potatoes carefully. Place in a preheated oven at 400° until a fork pierces them easily. Immediately wrap the potatoes in a dish towel until ready to serve (no more than 20 minutes). When ready to serve, cut a cross in each potato. Pinch the skins to expose the white of the potato. Serve with condiments.

Ski Slope Totes

On the slopes one can usually find ski-hut snack bars, but inevitably they are crowded, and the food mediocre and expensive. Instead fill a knapsack, dine atop your favorite hill or mountain and ski down hill with a full stomach and a lighter knapsack!

Menu

Thermos of cream of tomato soup
Skiers Submarine
Round celery
No-Bake cookies

Skier's Submarine

1 long, narrow loaf of French bread
6 slices of cheese (mozzarella or provolone)
3 slices of red onion, separated into rings
3 ripe tomatoes, sliced
6 slices of bologna

12 slices of salami
12 slices of cucumber
1 T. olive oil
1 T. wine vinegar
½ t. basil
½ t. oregano

Cut the bread in half lengthwise. Arrange next six ingredients evenly on one half of the cut loaf. Mix oil, vinegar, basil and oregano. Sprinkle the mixture over the sandwich filling. Top with the other half of the loaf. Slice into six servings and wrap in foil. Serves 6.

Round Celery

6 ribs of celery
3 oz. cream cheese
3 T. butter

3 oz. blue cheese
1 T. milk
Dash of Worcestershire sauce

Wash and dry celery. Cut celery into equal lengths. Mix next 5 ingredients. Stuff each rib of celery with mixture and "glue" ribs together to make 3 round celery stalks. Cut in half. Wrap in foil. Serves 6.

No-Bake Cookies

2 c. sugar   ½ c. milk
1 stick margarine

Boil the above together for one minute. Stir into the above mixture:

2 T. peanut butter   3 c. rolled oats
4 T. cocoa   1 t. vanilla
Pinch salt

Mix well and drop by teaspoon on waxed paper. Makes 2 dozen cookies.

Barbecue

Pack your banquet in old baskets lined with oil cloth placements (just cut oil cloth to appropriate size) and head to your favorite picnic sight. Don't forget the charcoal and lighter fluid. (A great time and space saver are the easy-light briquets that come loose like regular charcoal or in a solid pack. Available in your grocery.)

Menu

Hamburgers
Hot Dogs
Corn on the Cob
Grilled onions
Sliced tomatoes with basil or your favorite herb
Your favorite brownie mix

Hamburgers

Make your hamburgers and hot dogs before leaving on your picnic. Wrap in individual foil packages and put in a cooler. Remember there are countless ways to be creative about your hamburgers and hot dogs.

Basic Hamburger Recipe:
To each pound of hamburger add one small chopped onion, 1 egg and 1 t. chopped parsley. Mix well and shape into patties.

Variations:
1. After making the meat into patties, make a small depression in the center of each patty and fill with 1 T. blue cheese. Press the meat together to seal. Grill. Serve on toasted English muffins.
2. Make two thin patties per person. Place a slice of your favorite cheese on top of one patty. Cover with second patty. Press edges together. (Try pepper cheese or mozzarella cheese.)

Hot Dogs
1. Heat a can of chili on the grill. Spoon over hot dogs. Serve with chopped onions.
2. Score hot dogs with a sharp knife in several places. Marinate hot dogs in your favorite barbecue sauce for several hours. Grill, basting with the sauce.
3. Serve grilled hot dogs with horseradish, taco sauce, and different mustards for a change.

Grilled Corn on the Cob

1 or 2 ears of corn per person Salt
Lots of butter

Carefully pull back corn husk just enough to remove the corn silk. Put the husks back in place and tie end closed with a piece of string. Put the corn in a bucket of water until you are ready to grill. The corn absorbs the water which helps prevent it from burning. Grill the corn for ½ hour, turning frequently. Serve with lots of butter.

An easy way to serve butter for corn on the cob is to melt the butter in a pan on the grill. Each guest can apply the butter with a pastry brush.

Grilled Onions

One medium Spanish onion   Lots of butter
** per person   Salt and pepper**

Wrap each onion in heavy foil. There is no need to peel or remove the skins of the onions. Put the onions right on the coals as soon as you light the fire. Use a bit more charcoal since the onions need lots of heat. Cook for 55 minutes, turning occasionally. At serving time, open the foil and peel back the charred skin. Serve onion with butter.

Tailgate Picnic

Colorful oil cloth spread on a station wagon's tailgate, a wine carafe filled with roadside wildflowers and tied with ribbons of your favorite team's colors, and you are ready for a touchdown!

Menu

Thermos of Spinach Soup
Pita Bread Sandwiches
Carrot, celery and zucchini sticks sprinkled with lime juice
Apple Pie

Spinach Soup

2 packages of frozen, chopped spinach	2 T. parsley, minced
5 green onions, minced	2 qts. milk
	Cayenne pepper to taste

Thaw spinach; this takes a while so it is a good idea to let it thaw overnight. Squeeze as much of the water as possible from the spinach. Put spinach in a pan; add milk and heat for 5 minute. Saute onions and parsley in 1 T. butter until limp (5 minutes). Add to soup. Sprinkle a dash of cayenne into soup. Heat for 5 minutes and pour into a thermos. Serves 8.

Pita Bread Sandwiches

1 round pita (pocket bread) per serving	1 large onion, chopped
¼ head of lettuce, shredded	1 can black olives, chopped
1½ c. cheddar cheese, grated	½ lb. salami and
3 tomatoes	½ lb. pepperoni, diced and mixed
1 jar pepperoncini peppers, chopped	Mustards

Cut each pita in half and toast for 3-4 minutes at 400° or until crisp and hot. Wrap in foil immediately. Pack each of the next 7 ingredients in separate containers. Each guest fills his bread with a mixture of the ingredients and a dollop of mustard. Serves 8.

No Muss/No Fuss Apple Pie

1 ready-to-bake pie shell
6 apples, sliced, peeled and
  cored
Lemon juice

½ c. sugar mixed with
¼ c. flour and
1 t. cinnamon
½ pint sour cream
Additional cinnamon

Fill pie shell with apples. Sprinkle apples with lemon juice. Sprinkle sugar/flour/cinnamon mixture over apples. Spread sour cream over entire pie. Sprinkle additional cinnamon over sour cream for color. Bake at 375° for 40 minutes. Serves 8.

Picnic Essentials
Keep the following items in a basket so that you are always ready to go:

cork screw
can opener
sharp knife
handy wipes
aluminum foil
paper towels
insect repellent
paper cups and plates
napkins
plastic forks, knives, spoons
oil cloth for a table cloth
salt and pepper

Thanksgiving

Stephen Young, a Dartmouth graduate, wrote:

"Don't forget to include directions for roasting a turkey. Lots of students are left at school over Thanksgiving while their friends sun and ski. These waifs often band together to combat loneliness for a traditional Thanksgiving dinner. Nine times out of ten they haven't a clue about cooking turkeys . . ."

Menu

Turkey with dressing
Acorn Squash
Cranberries
Sweet Potatoes
Pumpkin Pie

Turkey with Dressing

Count on one pound of turkey per person. If the turkey is frozen, it takes 3 to 4 days to defrost in the refrigerator. Leave the turkey in its original wrapper until thawed. When thawed, remove the giblets from inside of the turkey. *Remember to keep the turkey refrigerated once thawed and cook within one day.*

Follow the directions on the Pepperidge Farm Stuffing Mix. Do add the suggestions of onion, celery, etc. for flavor.

Fill the turkey cavity with the dressing. Do not pack the cavity too tightly since stuffing tends to swell during cooking. Any extra dressing may be placed in a covered casserole and heated in the oven for 30 minutes at 350°.

Close the cavity openings with a skewer and place a meat thermometer in the thickest part of the thigh. Wrap the turkey in heavy foil and place in a roaster in a 325° oven.

The turkey is done when the thermometer reads 180-185°.

Timetable

Pounds	Hours @ 325°	Resting time
6-8	3½-4	20 min.
8-12	3¾ - 4½	20 min.
12-16	4-5	30 min.

Remove to a platter and discard skewers. Turkey should rest for at least 20 minutes before carving.

Acorn Squash

Plan on ½ squash per person. Cut squash in half. Scoop out seeds. Place squash in a pan cut side down. Fill pan with an inch of water. Place in a 325° oven for one hour. Remove squash from pan and turn right side up. Fill squash with 1 T. butter and 1 T. brown sugar per half. Return to the oven for 10 minutes or until butter is melted.

Sweet Potatoes

2-22 oz. cans of sweet potatoes, drained	¼ t. nutmeg
¾ c. butter	¼ t. cinnamon
¼ c. milk	Tiny marshmallows or
	½ c. pecans

Heat drained potatoes in a pan. Whip butter, milk and seasonings. Put into a casserole and sprinkle with marshmallows or pecans. Bake at 325° for 30 minutes. Serves 8.

Pumpkin Pie

There are many good "heat and serve" pumpkin pies available in your grocery, particularly around the holidays. Warm in a 325° oven while enjoying your dinner.

Afternoon Tea
for Your Roommate's Birthday

Decorate with your roommate in mind: balloons in school colors tied everywhere, a huge banner proclaiming the event strung in an obvious place and favorite music on the stereo.

Menu

Friendship Tea
Chocolate Birthday Cake

Friendship Tea

This tea is good to have on hand for every occasion, including a bad cold, final exams or your roomie's special day.

1 c. Tang	½ c. instant tea
1 c. sugar	½ t. cinnamon
1 pkg. lemonade mix	¼ c. ground cloves
(found in grocery)	1 t. dried oregano

Mix all ingredients and store in a jar. Add two teaspoons to each cup of boiling water. It is wonderful cold, too!

Chocolate Cake

½ c. butter or margarine	1 can chocolate syrup
1 c. sugar	(16 oz.)
4 eggs	1 t. vanilla
	1 c. self-rising flour

Cream the butter and sugar until smooth. Add eggs, one at a time, beating well after each one with an electric mixer. Add chocolate syrup and vanilla. Beat in flour. Pour into a 9x13 pan which has been greased and floured. Bake at 350° for 45-50 minutes. Cool. Sprinkle with powdered sugar. Serves 8.

Final Snacks

When cramming for those all-important finals, avoid stimulants such as too much caffine! Try some nourishing snacks such as:

Mid-Term Soup

1 large can V-8 juice	3 T. minced celery
3 T. minced green pepper	6 T. Parmesan cheese

Heat juice; do not boil. Add pepper and celery. Simmer for 10 minutes. Sprinkle with cheese. Serves 6.

Fruits, Nuts and Grains

1 18 oz. box quick cooking oats	1 c. chopped dried apricots
	¼ c. chopped dried pecans
½ c. brown sugar	1 c. raisins
1 c. non-fat skim dried milk	1 c. chopped mixed nuts

Combine and put into an air-tight jar or container. For cereal, just add some milk and let stand for one hour, or cook with milk for 6 minutes and serve warm. Good for one week's worth of heavy studying!

Griz-zies

½ c. margarine	½ c. mixed nuts
1 t. curry powder or	1½ c. rice, wheat or corn chex
1 t. garlic salt	or a combination of all
1 c. pretzel sticks	1 t. Worcestershire sauce

Melt butter in a shallow pan in a 375° oven. Stir in curry powder or garlic salt and Worcestershire sauce. Toss in remaining ingredients. Cook in oven for an additional 5 minutes. The above recipe will get you though one art history final or three chapters of Frazer's *The Golden Bough*.

Tunaburgers

Your favorite recipe for tuna   1 c. grated cheddar or Swiss
   salad for 4 people   cheese
                          4 hot dog or hamburger buns

Add cheese to tuna recipe. Fill the buns. Wrap individually in foil and heat in a 325° oven for 20-25 minutes or heat on a grill until cheese melts.

Popcorn

Popcorn is a nutritious snack. Toss with Parmesan cheese after popping for a different taste.

INDEX

119

Yes, I want my recipe in the next *College Cookbook.*

STUDENT'S NAME

UNIVERSITY

ADDRESS

RECIPE ENCLOSED

**Mail to: The College Cookbook
7714 Woodway, Dept. C,
Houston, Texas 77063**

Yes, I want my recipe in the next *College Cookbook.*

STUDENT'S NAME

UNIVERSITY

ADDRESS

RECIPE ENCLOSED

**Mail to: The College Cookbook
7714 Woodway, Dept. C,
Houston, Texas 77063**

Yes, I want my recipe in the next *College Cookbook.*

STUDENT'S NAME

UNIVERSITY

ADDRESS

RECIPE ENCLOSED

**Mail to: The College Cookbook
7714 Woodway, Dept. C,
Houston, Texas 77063**